Making
SCIENCE
CURRICULUM
Matter

Making SCIENCE CURRICULUM Matter

Wisdom for the Reform Road Ahead

Barbara Brauner Berns
Judith Opert Sandler
Editors

A JOINT PUBLICATION

Copyright © 2009 by Education Development Center, Inc.

All rights reserved. When forms and sample documents are included, their use is authorized only by educators, local school sites, and/or noncommercial or nonprofit entities that have purchased the book. Except for that usage, no part of this book may be reproduced or utilized in any form or by any means, electronic or mechanical, including photocopying, recording, or by any information storage and retrieval system, without permission in writing from the publisher.

For information:

Corwin Press
A SAGE Company
2455 Teller Road
Thousand Oaks, California 91320
www.corwinpress.com

SAGE India Pvt. Ltd.
B 1/I 1 Mohan Cooperative
 Industrial Area
Mathura Road, New Delhi 110 044
India

SAGE Ltd.
1 Oliver's Yard
55 City Road
London EC1Y 1SP
United Kingdom

SAGE Asia-Pacific Pte. Ltd.
33 Pekin Street #02-01
Far East Square
Singapore 048763

Library of Congress Cataloging-in-Publication Data

Making science curriculum matter: wisdom for the reform road ahead / Barbara Brauner Berns and Judith Opert Sandler, editors
    p. cm.
"A joint publication with Education Development Center, Inc."
Includes bibliographical references and index.
ISBN 978-1-4129-6722-8 (cloth)
ISBN 978-1-4129-6723-5 (pbk.)

  1. Science—Study and teaching (Elementary)—United States. 2. Science—Study and teaching (Secondary)—United States. I. Berns, Barbara Brauner. II. Sandler, Judith Opert. III. Title.

LB1585.3.M357 2009
372.3'5043—dc22   2008009172

08 09 10 11 12   10 9 8 7 6 5 4 3 2 1

Acquisitions Editor:	Dan Alpert
Editorial Assistant:	Tatiana Richards
Production Editor:	Jane Haenel
Copy Editor:	Cheryl Rivard
Typesetter:	C&M Digitals (P) Ltd.
Proofreader:	Anne Rogers
Indexer:	Michael Ferreira
Cover Designer:	Rose Storey
Graphic Designer:	Lisa Riley

Contents

Foreword: Showing the Way to Stronger Science Teaching and Learning by *Janice Earle* — vii

Acknowledgments — xi

1. Introduction by *Millicent Lawton, Barbara Brauner Berns, and Judith Opert Sandler* — 1

2. Putting Curriculum at the Center of Science Education Reform by *Millicent Lawton, Barbara Brauner Berns, and Judith Opert Sandler* — 7
    Curriculum in the Spotlight — 9
    Fully Realizing Science Standards — 12
    A New Era in Science Education Materials — 14
    Helping Schools Focus on a Richer Curriculum — 17
    Summary and Conclusion — 21

3. Selecting Curriculum Materials: A Critical Step in Science Program Design by *Joseph A. Taylor* — 23
    Creating a Thoughtful Selection Process — 25
    Building the Foundation for a Successful Selection Process — 30
    Summary and Conclusion — 33

4. Professional Development for Curriculum Awareness Adoption, and Implementation by *Nancy M. Landes* — 35
    Building on Professional Development Research — 37
    Addressing Professional Development Challenges — 42
    Summary and Conclusion — 46

5. The Role of Assessments and Accountability
    by *Sally Goetz Shuler, Judi Backman, and Steve Olson* — 49
    Supporting New Frontiers in Classroom Assessment — 51
    Navigating the Straits of Accountability Testing — 55
    Summary and Conclusion — 59

6. Lessons Learned From Evaluation *by Katrina Laguarda*   **61**
    Different Strategies, Different Settings   62
    Building Demand, Offering Help   63
    Insight Into Adoption of Curriculum Materials   65
    Promising Signs for Adoption and Implementation   68
    Barriers to Adoption and Implementation   69
    Identifying Regional Capacity   70
    Summary and Conclusion   72

7. Using the Centers' Work to Improve Science Education: Some Practical Advice *by Millicent Lawton, Barbara Brauner Berns, and Judith Opert Sandler*   **75**
    Getting Down to Business: Seeking Support   77
    Addressing Substance: Action Steps   78
    Addressing Support: Action Steps   80
    Connecting With Research   83
    Being Aware of the Context   84
    Summary and Conclusion   85

Appendix I. Standards-Based Curriculum Materials Disseminated by EDC's K–12 Science Center   **87**

Appendix II. EDC's K–12 Science Center's Curriculum Selection and Curriculum Evaluation Process   **95**

Appendix III. IMPACT Curriculum Review Panel MST Instructional Materials Evaluation Tool   **99**

References and Further Reading   **111**

Index   **117**

Foreword

Showing the Way to Stronger Science Teaching and Learning

Since its inception in 1950, the National Science Foundation (NSF), through the Directorate for Education and Human Resources, has supported the development of instructional materials for students. In the 1990s, a confluence of factors led to the funding and creation of centers located around the country to promote familiarity with and use of rigorous curriculum materials in mathematics and science. This book describes the work of the four NSF-funded dissemination and implementation centers that focused on science curriculum.

The first factor in the creation of the centers was the advent of national standards defining what all students should know and be able to do, starting with those from the National Council of Teachers of Mathematics and *Science for All Americans* from the American Association for the Advancement of Science, both in 1989, and the National Research Council's *National Science Education Standards* in 1996. In 1991, the NSF's Division of Elementary, Secondary, and Informal Education requested the development of multiyear mathematics materials that incorporated the standards. Comprehensive science materials that reflected the standards from that subject area followed. The national standards led to increased activity at both the state and district levels, and many states created or revised their own standards based on, at least in part, the national documents. During this time, the NSF was also moving forward with systemic reform initiatives—the Statewide Systemic Initiative program, the Urban Systemic Initiative program, and the Local Systemic Change program. Collectively, these systemic efforts were encouraging districts and states to examine and make more-coherent curricula, professional development, assessment, partnerships, and policy. Many of the systemic projects centered their interventions on curriculum reform with associated professional development.

The idea of funding new centers to provide states and districts with targeted assistance in curriculum adoption and implementation began in earnest with recommendations that came out of the Instructional Materials Development (IMD) program, which was designed to generate the exemplary instructional materials delivering science education in line with the national standards. Reviews of that program found "considerable slippage between marketing, adoption, and use of the materials." Interviews and studies concluded that "sustained professional development is a necessary accompaniment to successful implementation of IMD products." Looking at the IMD program pushed the NSF to think in terms of more support for districts or schools implementing exemplary materials. Exemplary curriculum is often challenging for teachers, because it requires deeper content knowledge in science. It may use technology in challenging ways to enhance learning. In short, a new kind of curriculum material presents a long list of both important opportunities and practical challenges.

By 1996, the work of the dissemination and implementation (D&I) centers, the heart of this book, was about to begin. In more formal terms, the NSF's Division of Elementary, Secondary, and Informal Education requested projects that integrated the use of instructional materials with teacher training, assessment, computer and telecommunication needs, and general resource requirements. From 1997 to 1999, the centers were launched with funds from both the IMD and Teacher Enhancement programs.

The key ideas behind the D&I projects were to get research-based curricula into wider use and to help educators see the potential for an exemplary science curriculum to reshape how schools teach and what students learn. There was no requirement that the materials be developed through NSF funds, nor was there a definition of "research-based" that appeared in the solicitations. However, inside the NSF, the general model used in the IMD program was accepted as the template. That is, materials were developed based on current research on teaching and learning by teams of disciplinary experts and educators. After development, pilot-testing and revision occurred. A period of field-testing and revision followed, to help ensure that the materials could be successfully used with diverse populations of teachers and students.

The program solicitations sought projects that were national or multistate in scope. Funds were offered for 3 to 5 years. Over the lives of the grants, the projects were asked to address some or all of the following:

- Assistance in determining the critical local factors entering into the selection and adoption of the instructional materials
- Assistance in assessing the alignment of the instructional materials with national standards and school, district, and/or state curricular frameworks
- Assistance in assessing the alignment of instructional materials across grade levels and, as appropriate, between science and mathematics
- Planning of professional development that prepares and supports teachers in the use of the instructional materials
- Identification and development of tools (professional development materials, assessment packages, resource guides) that support the necessary teacher enhancement
- Strategies to identify and build the partnerships needed to support school change that enables the adoption and implementation of exemplary instructional materials
- Minor revisions to instructional materials, as appropriate, that facilitate articulation between grade levels
- Enhancement of potential staff developers in the implementation of the curricular materials
- Assistance in determining the critical factors needed to make decisions about appropriate educational technologies and student assessments to implement the new instructional materials

All programs leave some legacy. The D&I centers helped many schools and districts, from remote rural areas to major urban centers, to change how they defined the goals of their science education program and the materials and methods they used to bring science to life for their students. This book will no doubt be another part of the centers' legacy, as it gathers the key experiences and lessons of this initiative and presents them for others to use in continuing to open the way for an engaging, challenging science curriculum that will help students grasp and appreciate how the world works.

Janice Earle
Senior Program Director
National Science Foundation
Arlington, Virginia

Acknowledgments

The Center for Science Education at Education Development Center, Inc. (EDC), in Newton, Massachusetts, oversaw the writing and editing of this book, extending the legacy of EDC's K–12 Science Curriculum Dissemination Center. However, we could not have done so without a wonderful group of collaborators. We thank our own staff as well as colleagues and writing partners from the three other science curriculum dissemination and implementation centers described in this book: the IMPACT Center at the Center for the Enhancement of Science and Mathematics Education at Northeastern University in Boston; the K–8 Leadership and Assistance for Science Education Reform centers, based at the National Science Resources Center in Washington, D.C.; and the Science Curriculum Implementation Center at Biological Sciences Curriculum Study (BSCS) in Colorado Springs, Colorado. We want to acknowledge the contribution of EDC's external evaluator, Policy Studies Associates (PSA) in Washington, D.C. Specifically, we thank those individuals whose ideas and hard work gave the manuscript life: Judi Bachman, Marilyn Decker, Claire Duggan, Katrina Laguarda, Nancy Landes, Sally Shuler, and Joe Taylor. Let us also mention that the writing and editing of Lonnie Harp and Millicent Lawton united the book into a cohesive whole.

We offer our thanks to the National Science Foundation, which made this project possible. Our NSF program officer, Janice Earle, was the first to envision the book, and her leadership ensured that it came to fruition.

In addition, we appreciate the candor and wisdom of those who participated in the symposium "Curriculum as the Leading Edge of Reform: The Building of Capacity and Leadership by the Science Curriculum Dissemination Centers" on May 17–18, 2006, in Baltimore. The symposium, also funded by the NSF, served as an incubator for the writing of the book. The attendee list is too long to recount here, but everyone who took part contributed in some way to this book.

And most of all, we want to mention the thousands of science educators from across the country who exhibited such a strong commitment to improving science education for the students in their classrooms and schools. Teachers, curriculum specialists, and administrators participated in all venues of professional development, consulted with center staff, shared their experiences and challenges with colleagues, and informed the development of many of the resources and learnings that appear in this book. Without them, none of this would have been possible!

Barbara Brauner Berns

Judith Opert Sandler

Publisher's Acknowledgments

Corwin Press would like to acknowledge the contributions of the following individuals:

Polly BeeBout
Teacher (Science)
CY Junior High School
Casper, WY

Joe Bellina
Professor of Physics
Saint Mary's College
Notre Dame, IN

Sandra K. Enger
Associate Professor of Science Education
The University of Alabama, Huntsville
Huntsville, AL

Jenny Sue Flannagan
Assistant Professor and Director
Martinson Center for Mathematics and Science,
    Regent University
Virginia Beach, VA

Susan Koba
Science Education Consultant
Retired
Omaha, NE

J-Petrina McCarty-Puhl
Secondary Science Teacher
Robert McQueen High School
Reno, NV

Melissa Miller
Teacher (6th Grade)/Science and Mathematics Chair
Lynch Middle School
Farmington, AR

Ben Sayler
Director
Center for the Advancement of Mathematics and Science Education
Black Hills State University
Spearfish, SD

1

Introduction

*Millicent Lawton, Barbara Brauner Berns,
and Judith Opert Sandler*

Education Development Center, Inc.

Without question, the education of America's students in science, from kindergarten through Grade 12, stands at a critical crossroads. The generally inadequate outcomes from science teaching and learning in recent years are well documented on both national and international testing yardsticks: too many students have neither the skills nor the understanding in science to enable them to compete in the increasingly scientific and technically oriented global workplace or to successfully pursue higher education in science or science education. (Certainly, there are pockets of excellence now, but, overall, students' science education experiences are uneven and inequitable.)

Looking forward, there are really just three choices: (1) maintain the status quo; (2) provide additional resources, but for uncoordinated, quick-fix efforts; or (3) pull together as a nation and undertake a comprehensive overhaul, a coordinated refocusing and reinvigoration, of precollegiate science education.

The first option would yield predictable results, allowing the current situation to prevail and perpetuating the shortcomings that are not only unsatisfying to educators (and everyone else) but unjust to students and damaging to the American economy and its global competitiveness. The second option provides some movement forward, but usually for a short time and serving only as a stopgap, again shortchanging all involved. The third option, on the other hand, would enable the United States to claim international excellence: Well-qualified teachers would receive the support and training they need, teach a rich curriculum and assess learning so that students develop critical-thinking and problem-solving skills, and impart to students a lifelong understanding of how the world works.

Which path our nation takes from this crossroads remains to be seen. The authors certainly hope that it is the latter, and that is why we have written this book at this time. Our book is intended to assist those who wish to pursue that third option: doing right by our students, our teachers, and our country in science education by focusing on curricula.

There are reasons for optimism. Today, there is an energetic discussion about education and a renewed sense of urgency around reforms to science education. The following are some examples:

- The federal No Child Left Behind (NCLB) education law's requirement for state testing in science went into effect with the 2007–2008 school year, ideally prompting schools who had left science behind (in favor of reading and mathematics) to go back and get it. For those who rarely targeted science, there may be a new momentum to begin building a science program.
- The congressional reauthorization of NCLB, under way as this book goes to press, will help set the agenda for science education in the near future, including matters of standardized testing and accountability measures for schools.
- Several national reports have recently called for immediate attention to improving precollegiate science education, including the National Academy of Sciences' study of U.S. economic competitiveness, *Rising Above the Gathering Storm*.
- There is an ongoing policy debate about whether national education standards should supplant the existing system of academic standards decided state by state.
- The 2008 presidential campaign and election mean education appears as a topic on candidates' campaign platforms and policy agendas, if not always seen as a priority.

Finally—and frustratingly—there is hope for change because we already know that things need not be as they are. There exist many resources in the science education field—from research to instructional materials to professional development programs—that could help facilitate the turnaround that is so desperately needed. In short, we know what to do; we just haven't done it.

Where should science education reform start? Our experience tells us that the curriculum enacted in the classroom is "ground zero" for changing the way science is taught and learned in this country.

So, with the public-policy spotlight trained on science education, yet with the apparent need for clearer direction, this book relates our experiences pursuing systemic science education reform, K–12, through the dissemination and use of standards- and research-based curriculum materials.

Specifically, this book represents the collective experiences of half of the eight "dissemination and implementation" centers that were funded by the National Science Foundation (NSF), begun between 1997 and 1999, to foster the understanding and use of exemplary mathematics and science instructional materials. Four centers were created to focus on math instructional materials exclusively, three were funded to do the same for science materials only, and one dealt with both subject areas. This book covers the activities of the latter four centers' work in science.

The science curriculum centers were based at research and development organizations, colleges, and universities around the country; namely, Biological Sciences Curriculum Study (BSCS) in Colorado Springs, Colorado; Education Development Center, Inc., in Newton, Massachusetts; the National Science Resources Center in Washington, D.C.; and Northeastern University in Boston. The initial NSF grants were for 3 or 5 years, but supplementary funding kept some of the work going for nearly a decade.

We think our perspective is worthwhile because when the NSF made the commitment to invest in improving science education nationally in this way, it turned to these four science curriculum centers, each with a depth of expertise in the field.

The NSF work was a cutting-edge experiment, and the centers were essentially national truth seekers. The idea was both to figure out how best to assist schools, districts, and states in using exemplary standards-based instructional materials (whether the materials were funded by the NSF or not) and to glean lessons from that work that might benefit the field.

Frequently, education reformers are urged not to "reinvent the wheel"—that is, not to attempt an innovation in a way that is uninformed by previous efforts. Instead, the advice goes, they should learn from the wisdom of others' past experiences to make the most efficient use of time, money, and people—and to have the best chance of achieving positive change. That kind of wisdom is exactly what this book strives to impart.

This book does not have all the answers, by any stretch of the imagination; indeed, the authors have learned the hard way that there is no "magic bullet" or series of recipe-like steps to follow toward making science education better and more in tune with standards and research. However, our experiences—the failures and the successes—can and should help shape the national discourse and influence action plans for improving science education.

Despite the existence of federal education laws and national policy debates, most education decisions in this country are still made at the state and local levels. Therefore, the members of your education community are the people who—if they choose to join the cause of making U.S. science education a global exemplar—will be the decision makers. The focus of their efforts should be science curriculum. That means you, the reader, can have a hand in bringing the lessons in this book to bear on the classroom level.

The classroom: That's where curriculum matters. And that curriculum needs to have certain features. It needs to be standards and research based as well as scientifically accurate, developmentally appropriate, and pedagogically sound. In addition, curriculum does not exist in a vacuum. Attention must be paid to the local context, and care must be given to its implementation, such as aligning it with comprehensive assessments and professional development.

For future science education reformers, this book explains that the necessary work is multifaceted, demanding, and nuanced and that it requires strong support, inside and outside the school community. It highlights the need, among other points, to build capacity among people and institutions for accepting and using curriculum as a driver of other science education improvements and to create a network of outside partners and an infrastructure for the improvement of science education, from the local to the national level.

This book's Chapter 2 provides some context for the work of the centers and describes their mission, while Chapter 3 focuses on efforts to build a more meaningful and productive curriculum selection process. The ways that professional development was used to advance and complement the curriculum materials are discussed in Chapter 4, and Chapter 5 outlines challenges associated with assessment—changes necessary inside classrooms and the pressure exerted by state and federal accountability programs. The evaluations of the centers are summarized in Chapter 6, and the final chapter, Chapter 7, discusses practical advice gleaned from the centers' work.

Who will best benefit from the curriculum-centered science education reform experiences described in this book? Most likely, those persons in school districts or state education departments who make decisions about curriculum, instruction, professional development, or assessment—or who serve on textbook selection committees. Others might also include, but are not limited to, science education coordinators, department heads, or directors at the district or state levels; superintendents; principals; teacher leaders; school board members; college and university science, science education, and curriculum faculty; leaders of science education initiatives within the professional science community; and business and community leaders.

In this book, we have done our part to convey our hard-won wisdom, our lessons learned, to help others pursue the "third option" of giving our nation the high-quality precollegiate science education it deserves. The rest is up to you.

2

Putting Curriculum at the Center of Science Education Reform

Millicent Lawton, Barbara Brauner Berns, and Judith Opert Sandler

Education Development Center, Inc.

In October 1996, the Third International Mathematics and Science Study (TIMSS) offered a sobering picture of the state of science education. Although U.S. fourth graders scored near the top of an international science test administered in 1994–1995, behind only Korea and Japan, the story got bleaker as it compared older students. U.S. eighth graders ranked in the middle of the international pack, noticeably behind top scorers in Singapore, Korea, and Japan as well as in several European nations. U.S. high school students scored even lower, significantly behind the international average. The results painted an unsettling picture of an international race to produce young adults competent in science know-how and skills.

For some, the news may have stopped with the international test comparisons. The TIMSS data, however, went further. Researchers found a major difference in science education between U.S. schools and those scoring at the top of the international comparisons: American science classes covered a wide range of topics but often provided students with only a shallow understanding of science when compared with top-scoring international schools. High-performing students from those countries tackled advanced biology and advanced physics concepts more often than U.S. students. The report described the U.S. curriculum as "a mile wide and an inch deep." TIMSS researchers urged a major review of how American schools teach science, from the topics covered to the skills students are expected to attain.

The TIMSS report arrived on the education reform scene about the same time as national standards in science education. Released in 1996 by the National Research Council after 4 years of deliberation, the *National Science Education Standards* clarified academic expectations for students, teachers, and school administrators. The voluntary U.S. standards defined the essentials of physical science, life science, earth and space science, and science and technology. The materials also went beyond the basic content to spell out expectations for student learning in science as inquiry, the history and nature of science, science in personal and social perspective, and unifying concepts and processes.

Almost a decade before the standards and TIMSS report were released, the National Science Foundation (NSF) had resumed its work developing exemplary instructional materials for science classes. In 1996–1997, in the wake of standards and the international comparisons, the NSF launched a program to create curriculum dissemination and implementation centers to expand educators' awareness and use of the standards-based materials. The centers would put curriculum at the core of wider efforts to improve teaching and learning and, consequently, give students a stronger education. As reform leaders talked about the need for "systemic" changes, the new centers were envisioned as a way to put stronger currricula and instructional materials at the heart of a major effort to significantly improve the way science would be taught and learned in schools.

At the time the centers opened for business, between 1997 and 1999, there was essentially no knowledge in the field about what it would take to attract the attention of diverse school districts nationwide and gain their commitment to exemplary, cutting-edge science curricula and their complementary systemic reforms. Now, a decade later, there is a record of those struggles and successes—and just at the right time. The need for guidance on how to improve science education is not only still present, but it is all the more urgent. A federal mandate for states to test students in science during their elementary, middle, and high school years has recently gone into effect. The law that instituted that requirement, the No Child Left Behind Act of 2001, is being reauthorized and could require that science test results count toward judgments of schools' annual progress (as the results of reading and mathematics tests do now).

> **TIMSS and NAEP Science Achievement:
> Reflecting Curriculum and Instruction**
>
> No measurable changes were detected in the average mathematics and science scores of U.S. fourth graders in the 8 years between the 1995 and 2003 TIMSS exams. American eighth graders moved above the international average in science and improved their standing against other countries but still trailed several Asian countries. Another measure of the nation's achievement in science, the National Assessment of Educational Progress (NAEP), found in 2005 that only 18% of U.S. high school seniors scored proficient or better. National scores on NAEP improved for fourth graders from 1996 to 2005, stayed unchanged at eighth grade, and declined over the period for 12th grade.
>
> Following the release of results from each of these two exams, experts and officials faulted both curriculum and instruction in the United States. The science and math material taught in American schools was neither rigorous enough nor organized in ways most helpful for student learning, they said. It was also too inconsistent across states and school districts. In addition, the scores reflected difficulty in recruiting teaching candidates, especially those with math and science content expertise, experts said, arguing that the nation also needed to do a better job of providing professional development for teachers.

Curriculum in the Spotlight

Education standards that, for the first time, defined what students should know and be able to do placed a new focus on the central role of curriculum. Although the general term *curriculum* can mean many things—from a syllabus to a textbook, and from the material teachers intend to teach to what students actually learn—organizers of the NSF initiative focused on what had come to be known as the "intended" curriculum. The term attempted to capture the basic concepts and materials organized to define a course or subject. Teachers now adapt materials to classroom situations and student needs and apply their own knowledge and energy to create a "delivered" curriculum. In this book, the terms *curriculum, curriculum materials*, and *instructional materials* are used interchangeably.

Researchers saw curriculum as an essential entry point to systemic reform and as a key weakness in lackluster science literacy and achievement levels. Even in the 1970s, researchers studying national math results concluded that strengths and weaknesses in instructional materials translated into what students did and didn't know. Other researchers also pointed to instructional materials as a decisive force in the direction of schools and student learning. "Unlike frameworks, objectives, assessments and other mechanisms that seek to guide curriculum, instructional materials are concrete and daily. They are the stuff of lessons and units, of what teachers and students do.... Not only are curriculum materials well-positioned to influence individual teachers' work but, unlike many other innovations, textbooks are already 'scaled up' and part of the routine of schools. They have 'reach' in the system," wrote researchers Ball and Cohen in 1996.

Researchers from TIMSS (now known as the Trends in International Mathematics and Science Study) reached similar conclusions. Analyses of scores and science materials from the countries involved in the math and science study "demonstrated the central role the textbook plays in setting U.S. content priorities for the allocation of teacher time to various topics as well as to the relative gains in achievement for these different topic areas," William H. Schmidt of Michigan State University found in 2003. His curriculum analysis from the 1995 study showed that U.S. science materials lacked focus, with the number and variety of topics that schools planned to cover so large that no science concepts could be treated in great depth. He also stated that compared with high-scoring countries, U.S. curriculum and instructional materials seemed like "laundry lists of unrelated ideas" instead of helping students see the coherent themes of the discipline. He said that the results also suggested the need for closer alignment between assessment and content standards and that higher performance standards needed to be created. "High academic standards require students to reason, analyze and develop problem-solving approaches and to make appropriate decisions through data collection and analysis," Schmidt stated in recommendations forwarded to federal lawmakers.

Such reports and arguments made a clear case for overhauling curriculum as a first step in improving science teaching and learning. Beyond seeing instructional materials as a driving force that could define how classrooms approach a subject, organizers of the NSF initiative saw a more engaging and rigorous curriculum as a centerpiece that schools and districts could use to redefine professional development and classroom assessment. A focus on curriculum and instructional materials could also transform textbook adoption and the process for selecting materials into an important learning opportunity. The process could become a way for teachers and administrators—even parents and communities—to seriously discuss expectations for science learning and a school's philosophy of education.

The NSF's Instructional Materials Development (IMD) projects were designed to create curriculum materials and student assessments that would move beyond traditional tests and textbooks to remake classroom instruction, helping students acquire a more sophisticated understanding of science content, higher-order thinking skills, and problem-solving abilities. The materials were designed to incorporate investigative, hands-on science education activities and align with national standards.

Projects ranged from major revisions and implementation of existing materials to the creation of entirely new ones, from a few modules at a single instructional level to comprehensive curricula for several school years, from a focus on a single subject to the integration of several disciplines, and from assessments embedded in classroom materials to the creation of assessment items and full programs that could be used by a school district or state. All projects included comprehensive national dissemination plans to ensure use of the materials in numerous and diverse settings. The project included funding for implementation sites to assist interested districts in the selection and classroom implementation of curricula.

In January 1997, the NSF spelled out the basic goals of its dissemination and implementation projects in its guidelines for proposals for centers that would focus on science and math. The explanation showed the central role envisioned for curriculum in shaping professional development, assessment, and the way schools and districts defined their approach to science education: "Science and mathematics education reform requires classroom implementation of high-quality, standards-based instructional materials, together with a comprehensive program of professional development for teachers and the alignment of school district policy, practice and resources."

A Science Education Reform Time Line

1986—The National Science Foundation launches its TRIAD program to create an exemplary elementary science curriculum. The program is the forerunner of the Instructional Materials Development program supporting curriculum development.

February 1989—The American Association for the Advancement of Science publishes *Science for All Americans*, outlining what students should know in science, mathematics, and technology.

December 1995—The National Research Council issues the first printing of its 1996 publication, *National Science Education Standards*.

October 1996—Results of the Third International Mathematics and Science Study show gaps between U.S. fourth, eighth, and 12th graders and their international peers. Subsequent results were reported in 1999 and 2003.

(Continued)

> (Continued)
>
> **January 1997**—The NSF publishes its call for proposals for dissemination and implementation centers to focus on expanding the use of inquiry-based science materials.
>
> **1997–2001**—The NSF funds four dissemination and implementation centers focused on science curriculum.
>
> **January 2002**—President George W. Bush signs the No Child Left Behind Act of 2001, holding schools accountable for student test performance and achievement gaps in academic subjects, including reading, mathematics, and science.
>
> **2007**—Funding expires for the science curriculum dissemination and implementation centers.

Fully Realizing Science Standards

The national science education standards are often conveniently reduced to the catalog of topical issues that should be covered in elementary, middle, or high school classrooms—the particulars of earth science, physics, biology, or chemistry that should be packed into lesson plans. Other important topics covered in the 1996 standards routinely take a backseat. Areas hardest or impossible to pin down in large-scale testing, such as designing or analyzing an investigation or developing teachers' theoretical knowledge, often fall by the wayside in discussions about implementing national standards. Although many traditional textbooks have been adapted to comply with the recommendations and claim to cover all the nuggets of science knowledge listed in the national science standards, the "standards-based" materials at the heart of the NSF program and the subject of the dissemination and implementation centers' work captured the larger view of science standards.

"Implementing the standards will require major changes in much of this country's science education," the authors of the national standards document wrote. "The standards rest on the premise that science is an active process. Learning science is something that students do, not something that is done to them. 'Hands-on' activities, while essential, are not enough. Students must have 'minds-on' experiences as well."

The text of the standards document continued: "The standards call for more than 'science as process,' in which students learn such skills as observing, inferring, and experimenting. Inquiry is central to science learning. When engaging in inquiry, students describe objects and events, ask questions, construct explanations, test those explanations against current scientific knowledge, and communicate their ideas to others. They identify their assumptions, use critical and logical thinking, and consider alternative explanations. In this way, students actively develop their understanding of science by combining scientific knowledge with reasoning and thinking skills."

The authors said that the science standards could "bring coordination, consistency and coherence to the improvement of science education." The document spelled out that a truly "standards-based" approach would involve teaching styles that create environments where teachers and students "work together as active learners." The standards addressed the need for professional development that provides teachers with "opportunities to develop theoretical and practical understanding and ability, not just technical proficiencies." The document also offered guidelines on assessment in science education programs: Assessment and learning are two sides of the same coin. Assessments provide an operational definition of standards, in that they define in measurable terms what teachers should teach and students should learn. The standards also stressed the need for science education programs throughout a child's schooling that build awareness and knowledge about big concepts like systems, order, and organization; evidence, models, and explanation; and more.

The NSF sought to fund the creation of instructional materials that would help teachers provide classroom experiences true to the standards' wide-ranging goals with extensive support. The dissemination and implementation centers would take the first step in building awareness about those materials and other research- and standards-based materials. The centers would help school districts move toward the standards-based materials and help local education leaders embrace the wider vision of science learning by also addressing professional development, assessment, and leadership capacity. "High-quality instruction will require a strong and robust system that has all of its components aligned toward the achievement of a standards-based vision of instruction," said a 2001 report on the dissemination and implementation centers by Inverness Research Associates. A 2000 NSF report on the program from WestEd and Abt Associates, Inc., described the influence of standards on the centers' work: "The IMD materials require teachers to adopt reform-oriented pedagogy that is far more student centered than teacher centered, more discovery and investigative than direct instruction, and more conceptual than rote" (Tushnet et al. 2000, p. 47). Much of the centers' work was built around helping teachers and administrators adapt to the new vision of science education. "The centers are helping districts build their own capacity to sustain a process of ongoing curricular improvement," the Inverness report noted. At the center of the effort were materials that presented science and science education in a different light than did traditional textbooks.

A New Era in Science Education Materials

The materials promoted through the NSF program and the centers' work were research and standards based, as well as pilot-tested and field-tested. They sought to urge students deeper into scientific concepts and thinking, with lessons that taught science in the same way it is practiced—through investigation and analysis. The materials, some full-year texts and lab guides and others designed to be supplements, also aimed to provide information and experiences developmentally appropriate for students and reflective of best practices in instruction and student learning. Some examples follow of representative curriculum materials promoted through the centers.

- *Insights: An Inquiry-Based Elementary School Science Curriculum*, developed by Education Development Center (EDC), Inc., and published by Kendall/Hunt Publishing Company, targeted students in Grades K–6 with 17 curriculum modules. Each module lasted 6 to 8 weeks, including experiences designed to be age appropriate for students in Grades K–1, 2–3, 4–5, or 6. Teachers could use the materials as a core curriculum or as a supplement to another program. In Grades 2–3, for example, a module on liquids offered a study of water, oil, and corn syrup to address concepts such as density, cohesion, viscosity, and color. The lessons also showed how liquids pour and take the shape of their containers and how solids interact with liquids by sinking or floating. Examples of other modules included "Circuits and Pathways," one of five modules for Grades 4–5, or "Balls and Ramps," one of four modules for Grades K–1. The curriculum package included a materials kit that provided supplies for 32 students and a teacher's guide that discussed the frameworks the curriculum was built around. *Insights* modules were designed to build on students' prior knowledge, experience, and strengths. Each module also covered assessment and offered extensions that would connect science knowledge to math, language arts, or other subjects. Both small- and large-group discussions were provided for in the modules, as well as the use of techniques to encourage students to record and analyze their work, including class charts and science notebooks.

- At the middle school level, *Science and Technology Concepts for Middle Schools*, or STC/MS, developed by the National Science Resources Center, included eight units for seventh and eighth graders covering life, earth, and physical sciences as well as technological design. The materials, published by the Carolina Biological Supply Company between 2000 and 2002, were designed to be two 1-year courses or four single-semester courses. A unit called "Catastrophic Events" utilized interest in natural disasters to introduce ideas such as atmospheric storms, earthquakes, volcanoes, plate tectonics, and use of global systems data. Students worked to discover patterns, make predictions, and develop and support theories about past events and possible future occurrences. Other units covered topics such as "Electric Circuits and Control Systems" and "Human Body Systems." The latter unit included a project that required students to research disorders and diseases and explore how they are cured or treated through medicine and health care. A teacher's guide, student guide, resource book, equipment, and materials were part of the program, as well as professional development modules for teachers.

- For high schools, *BSCS Biology: An Ecological Approach* offered a full-year high school biology course built around environmental and ecological issues. The teacher's edition suggested that half of the class time be dedicated to the nearly 15 lab investigations included. Developed by the Biological Sciences Curriculum Study (BSCS), a Colorado nonprofit corporation commissioned by the NSF in 1958, the 10th edition of the text was published in 2006 by Kendall/Hunt Publishing Company. The materials included a student text and teacher's edition, a student study guide, a resource book for teachers, and a computer test bank. The materials were organized around five basic environmental biology themes broken into chapters. The "Continuity in the Biosphere" section comprised chapters on cell continuity, reproduction, development, heredity, and evolution. The "Patterns in the Biosphere" section was made up of chapters on behavior, selection, and survival; ecosystems of the past; biomes around the world; aquatic ecosystems; and managing human-affected ecosystems. Many of the student investigations also encouraged students to initiate and design their own further study of the subject matter. The teacher's resources included guides showing how the materials were aligned with national science education standards and Project 2061's *Benchmarks for Science Literacy,* published by the American Association for the Advancement of Science (AAAS) in 1993.

The common thread among the promoted instructional materials was that they were created to embody the deeper experience in science education envisioned in the standards and the exemplary instruction that grew from research in areas such as multiple intelligences, authentic assessment, embedded professional development, and more. Such materials contrasted sharply with the leading U.S. science textbooks, according to the 2003 report by William Schmidt of Michigan State. The report compared eighth-grade NSF materials to the eighth-grade materials used in Japan, Singapore, Korea, and the Czech Republic, the top-scoring countries in the TIMSS results reported in 1996. Schmidt found that the NSF science materials examined were more rigorous than typical U.S. textbooks but still below the level of the top international materials. The NSF materials encouraged twice as much "hands-on" work by science students compared with popular U.S. textbooks but still did not focus on those kinds of projects as much as international materials did. Schmidt's report concluded, "The NSF set out in their support of the development of new mathematics and science instructional materials (textbooks) to stimulate the field to formulate fresh approaches to curriculum. That they have done. In science, especially, the NSF instructional materials focus much more heavily on expecting students to do more than learn facts by becoming engaged in hands-on activities such as designing, conducting and interpreting empirical studies."

The years covered by the NSF instructional materials project were ones of scrutiny of U.S. science textbooks. The AAAS Project 2061 announced in 1999 that no widely used science textbook for middle school science received a satisfactory ranking. "Most textbooks cover too many topics and don't develop any of them well," the group said. "All texts include many classroom activities that either are irrelevant to learning key science ideas or don't help students relate what they are doing to the underlying ideas." The Project 2061 analysis was partially funded by the NSF. Calling textbooks "the backbone of classroom instruction," Project 2061 leaders said that although curriculum materials may be scientifically accurate, they often fail to help teachers and students understand how to apply important science concepts.

> **Teacher Preparation Time in an Inquiry Science Classroom**
>
> A "frequently asked questions" handout from EDC's K–12 Science Curriculum Dissemination Center explained how classrooms built around promoting science inquiry contrast with traditional teaching strategies and materials: "All of the inquiry-based programs engage the students with materials. Many challenge students with questions to pursue and problems to solve. Some ask students to design their own investigations. Teachers who have little experience with managing materials and engaging students in inquiry will need to spend more time preparing inquiry-based lessons than would be necessary in a text-based program. The amount of time will vary depending on how the selected program structures and packages the use of materials." The handout went on to explain that as teachers become familiar with classroom work built around inquiry experiences, preparation would become easier and that the time involved was similar to the effort secondary teachers put into preparing conventional science labs. For more information, see http://cse.edc.org/products/pdfs/faqCurrSelection.pdf.

Helping Schools Focus on a Richer Curriculum

The NSF-funded dissemination and implementation centers developed their own strategies for spreading the use of standards-based materials, with each taking a different approach to a set of common goals:

- Building awareness of the NSF curriculum materials among school districts and education systems, including colleges of education
- Working with school districts to transform the textbook selection and adoption process into an experience in which educators focus on science education priorities, student learning, and necessary resources
- Assisting schools and districts through the implementation process, including helping teachers use new curricula as designed
- Increasing local curriculum leadership capacity to ensure that choosing and thoughtfully implementing curriculum becomes an internal function capable of sustaining itself

In school locations as diverse as Talladega, Alabama; Yakima, Washington; South Bend, Indiana; and Boston, Massachusetts, the centers worked with schools, district offices, colleges of education, and community and business groups to shape local discussions about science learning and standards-based curriculum. Each center's efforts encouraged educators and others involved in improving science education to take a new, more challenging path that started with curriculum. Mark St. John, president of Inverness Research Associates in Inverness, California, told the invited audience at the May 2006 symposium "Curriculum as the Leading Edge of Reform: The Building of Capacity and Leadership" by the Science Curriculum Dissemination Centers that the centers viewed curriculum as "the teacher" of a new approach to science education that becomes complete with strong implementation.

"Curriculum is the basis of instruction, but it is also an approach to building capacity for doing the work of improvement," St. John said at the NSF-sponsored meeting in Baltimore, Maryland. "The process of taking on curriculum, learning about it, figuring out how to implement it, designing professional development, getting coaches trained, and all of the other supports that need to be in place, is an extraordinary capacity-building effort for schools and communities. . . . To implement curriculum both requires capacity and generates capacity."

To get curriculum information out and to respond to the needs of participating districts and communities, the centers commonly linked with regional intermediaries familiar with participating districts. Although they took similar approaches, the four centers varied their strategies and focus:

• EDC's K–12 Science Curriculum Dissemination Center grew from within EDC's Center for Science Education, based in Newton, Massachusetts. EDC focused on building awareness and support for standards-based instructional materials in isolated or underserved school districts across the country through seminars, online courses, and resources and tools. EDC identified "hubs" around the country to house libraries of the exemplary materials and to support nearby communities and schools. Hubs serving a total of 500 school districts were located, at various times, in Chipley, Florida; Pueblo, Colorado; South Bend and Fort Wayne, Indiana; Moscow, Idaho; Clinton and Jackson, Mississippi; Petoskey and Traverse City, Michigan; Spearfish, South Dakota; Portland, Oregon; Dothan, Alabama; and Atlanta, Georgia. Through the hubs, participating district teams had access to customized technical assistance, including visits with expert users of the instructional materials, professional development sessions, referrals to resources, summer institutes, and electronic networking.

- The IMPACT New England Center was created by the Center for the Enhancement of Science and Mathematics Education (CESAME) at Northeastern University in Boston to build on existing regional work. Beyond Boston, IMPACT sites were established in Augusta, Maine; North Dartmouth and Shrewsbury, Massachusetts; Plymouth and Durham, New Hampshire; and Montpelier, Vermont. The center worked closely with state and regional K–12 science reform efforts, sharing exemplary teaching materials and curriculum expertise as well as working on professional development with school districts in the region. The center also provided Internet-based help and resources. Each satellite site, in turn, offered expertise to local schools or districts on planning and supporting local efforts. The regional sites networked with each other in addition to the Boston office, where they could tap more than 100 CESAME curriculum trainers who assisted in the project. The project also helped evaluate new and emerging curriculum reform programs to offer districts recommendations on materials and direction through an IMPACT Curriculum Review Panel.

- The National Science Resources Center, based in Washington, D.C., launched the Leadership and Assistance for Science Education Reform Center, known as the LASER Center. The group established regional centers that brought in a group of partners to help school districts that were examining the NSF project materials, with a focus on Grades K–8. The main regional centers were located in Alabama, California, Connecticut, Delaware, Oklahoma, Pennsylvania, Rhode Island, South Carolina, and Washington State, where nine regional alliances worked with about 100 school districts. Activities included Shared Vision conferences to bring together experts with local district officials to discuss challenges and issues. LASER also sponsored implementation academies and strategic planning institutes as part of a larger strategy of building reform awareness, initiating reform, implementing new programs, and developing leadership capacity. In addition to NSF funding, the LASER Center had a number of corporate sponsors with ties to science.

- The Science Curriculum Implementation Center at Biological Sciences Curriculum Study (BSCS) in Colorado Springs, Colorado, known as the SCI Center, focused on promoting high school–level curriculum materials but added middle school teams as districts broadened their reform efforts. Its work focused on the 3-year, intensive BSCS National Academy for Curriculum Leadership (NACL) program, which graduated two national cohorts of leadership teams. The teams included a key administrator (typically a district science supervisor), teachers, the principal, university representatives, representatives of a school-improvement program, and a representative of the business community. The SCI Center at BSCS incorporated awareness, selection, scaling up, and sustainability stages of implementation. The districts participating in the SCI Center's national cohorts included San Diego; Boston; Pittsburgh; Cincinnati; Harlan, Iowa; Linden, New Jersey; and a consortium of districts from the Ozark Rural Systemic Initiative centered in Webb City, Missouri. In 2004, the SCI Center at BSCS expanded the NACL to leadership teams from districts across Washington State, including Everett, Hockinson, Kennewick, La Center, North Thurston, Pasco, Puyallup, Richland, Selah, Sunnyside, Tacoma, Vancouver, Wishkah/North Beach, and Yakima, as well as teams from Delaware and California.

The need to significantly boost U.S. students' academic proficiency and scientific literacy served as an impetus for the creation of the NSF centers. However, promoting new, more rigorous instructional materials amounted to an uphill endeavor. Subsequent evaluations of the centers' work offer lessons from a wide range of districts, including some where teachers and administrators were completely new to inquiry-based science materials and teaching. Evaluations showed that although many educators were curious about the materials the centers promoted, only a fraction stayed with the project to attempt to significantly change how school systems consider or approach improving the quality of science education. One center reported that 523 districts participated in awareness-raising or planning activities, but only 123 ultimately used the materials.

The attempt to draw attention to the standards-based instructional materials came at a time when state accountability systems overwhelmingly focused on testing reading and math, especially at the elementary level, sometimes putting science on the back burner. Midway through the life of the centers, the federal No Child Left Behind law took effect, further increasing states' focus on reading and math achievement. Among other hurdles for elevating science education, many teachers' lack of science expertise and the division between aspects of science like biology, physics, chemistry, and earth or space science meant that few educators took an overarching view of the discipline. Meanwhile, observers characterized the curriculum selection routine in many districts as a "flip test" that involved skimming materials and usually favored familiar publishers and texts. Districts and schools traditionally devoted minimal time and resources to the selection process, often heavily influenced by the perks and pitches offered by large textbook publishers, particularly in larger districts. Beyond choosing materials, time and support for using them was a challenge in many schools, particularly when new curriculum marked a big change from the status quo. By contrast, the centers sought to build an infrastructure for thoughtful curriculum decision making and implementation.

However, in those districts that plowed ahead, evaluators found, inquiry-based materials often became the catalyst for improved teacher professional development, a more serious approach to textbook selection, and major changes in how students learn about science. In addition, many of the regional sites or hubs created by the centers profited from the project and outlived the program, using their added capacity and expertise to work on further science improvement efforts in local schools.

Summary and Conclusion

In the 1990s, the NSF was already funding the creation of materials consistent with the recently released science education standards, but the agency wanted to ensure that educators nationwide were aware of and would adopt and effectively use its materials, as well as other exemplary materials. To do so, it funded four science curriculum dissemination and implementation centers to provide information and support to regions, states, and districts, as well as build the capacity for ongoing reform. It was the NSF's vision that curriculum materials be the entry point for improvements in science education and the centerpiece around which systemic changes were made, including those to teacher professional development and ways of assessing student learning.

Standards-based instructional materials encouraged considerably more hands-on inquiry-based work by students than most schools were used to doing. In addition, the new materials were informed by research and had been improved through rigorous pilot-testing and field-testing prior to publication. In short, they were a major departure from the leading science textbooks, which, then as now, dominate the U.S. instructional materials market.

As the staff members of the four centers worked, it was not uncommon for them to encounter apathy, skepticism, or outright resistance—along with eager willingness—when they tried to promote these new, more rigorous materials. As evaluations of center work showed, only a fraction of the districts or educators who took part in events designed to raise awareness or encourage planning stuck with it long enough to enact change. However, those that did move forward found that inquiry-based materials could be powerful tools to catalyze impressive transformations in materials selection, professional development, and assessment.

Although the dissemination and implementation centers no longer operate as "formal centers" (the last of the NSF's funding extensions expired between 2005 and 2007), the centers' experiences offer valuable lessons about the potential areas for success—and pitfalls to avoid—for anyone trying to improve science teaching and learning.

3

Selecting Curriculum Materials

A Critical Step in Science Program Design

Joseph A. Taylor
Biological Sciences Curriculum Study

Getting innovative curriculum materials into science classrooms was the chief job of the dissemination and implementation centers funded by the National Science Foundation (NSF). The approach of all four centers grew from the belief that a serious understanding of the exemplary instructional materials could transform thinking and practice in schools.

National science education standards represent a landmark effort to define the essentials of physical science, life science, earth and space science, and science and technology. Beyond basic content, the national standards spell out expectations for student learning in the history and nature of science, science in personal and social perspective, science as inquiry, and unifying concepts and processes. As a result, curriculum materials developed with a vision of learning and teaching consistent with the national standards look much different from familiar and widely used materials that emphasize, for instance, the memorization of scientific terms.

The centers envisioned that the use of materials that encourage deeper, more active student thinking would be the centerpiece in a full reconsideration of professional development and classroom assessment as well as science teaching and learning. The first step involved making the curriculum selection process an opportunity for subject-area educators to hold serious discussions about expectations, teaching methods, standards, achievement data, and more in advance of thoughtful decisions about materials for science education.

Such a comprehensive approach to curriculum selection stood in stark contrast to the often haphazard, superficial, and opinion-based processes employed in many of the schools and districts. Familiar routines like the "flip test" or "thumb test" often prevailed, in which educators quickly scanned textbooks to get a cursory feel for basic organization, presentation, and colorful pictures or to look for favorite labs. Science teachers or district administrators often simply compared new materials with previously adopted textbooks to maintain familiarity. Quick impressions often topped selection criteria in a brief process lacking wide participation or serious discussion.

Curriculum developers try to design the best possible materials based on research and field-testing. The responsibility then lies with schools to make the most of these concepts and materials. The four science centers helped bridge that divide, building awareness and familiarity with the standards-based materials and showing educators how the centers offered a new way to enrich science education. But that was a constant challenge. Studies showed that although some of the innovative materials were well known, many were not. At best, the materials occupied a small, niche market driven by teachers active in professional groups like the National Science Teachers Association or district involvement with NSF grants. Most science department chairs said they were not interested in a major change in instructional materials and said they did not see any special connection between the materials the centers were promoting and achieving state-level science standards, according to studies by Inverness Research Associates.

Each center worked hard to develop a systematic, evidence-based selection process to assist teachers and administrators in making decisions about curriculum materials. These processes ranged from carefully selected guiding questions to graphic organizers with accompanying rubrics to analyze the content, instructional strategies, assessments, and support for teachers in a set of curriculum materials. Frequently, centers offered curriculum showcases and housed curriculum libraries, which gave educators firsthand exposure to the NSF-supported curricula and other standards-based curricula as a beginning step toward selection.

Table 3.1　Major Differences Between a Conventional K–12 Science Program and an Innovative Standards-Based Science Program

	Conventional	*Standards Based*
Role of student	Passive listener/ note-taker	Active observer, analyst, discussant
Role of teacher	Deliverer of content	Guide for student learning
Types of materials	Textbooks, worksheets, and formal labs	In-depth modules, featuring science notebooks, reading materials, etc.
Content of materials	Broad coverage; emphasis on facts and information	Deeper treatment of fewer topics; emphasis on understanding concepts, nature of science, and abilities of inquiry
Types of assessments	Multiple-choice or fill-in-the-blank at end of unit	Various formats (written, performance, observational, graphic, etc.) given continually

Creating a Thoughtful Selection Process

From the centers' perspective, the selection of curriculum materials required a clearly articulated process that included analysis of science content, student learning activities, teaching activities, teacher content information, and assessment strategies. These components were evaluated based on rubrics developed or adapted by the team members to meet local contexts and goals. In their work, the four centers each took their own approaches but followed common themes. They all encouraged a critique of current practice as a first step toward creating a climate for change, followed by the development of a common vision for the goals and strategies of science education.

Coaching District Teams Through the Selection Process

Through locations in Boston and six other sites in the region, school district teams affiliated with the IMPACT New England

Center were usually ushered through the selection process by a trained "implementation advisor," assigned after the team's first contact. That initial experience often included a visit to the center's curriculum resource center where educators could explore a variety of standards-based materials. The implementation advisors worked with districts to determine which standards-based curriculum might be the best match for local needs and then broker any help to support selection and implementation.

The IMPACT Center developed a selection rubric to help districts narrow their curriculum choices. The rubric included sections on student experiences, science content, organization and structure, teacher support materials, student assessment materials, and program development and implementation. (See Appendix III for the IMPACT rubric.)

Under the IMPACT rubric for student experiences, selection teams rated materials on a five-point scale on questions such as: "To what extent do students' experiences involve them in inquiry-based learning and problem solving (emphasize "doing" science or mathematics)?" Other questions in the section asked about multiple pathways to develop concepts and communicate ideas and solutions; the use of manipulatives or tools to explore, model, or analyze situations; fostering collaboration in the classroom; and more. Each question asked the selection team to cite evidence for their rating.

The IMPACT Center offered a series of implementation forums designed to explore implementation and sustainability issues. The forum topics included standards-based curriculum awareness, how to select and pilot curriculum materials, deepening science content, leadership for managing change, and more. When the selection team opted for standards-based materials, the IMPACT implementation advisor developed a formal implementation plan and turned to a pool of curriculum trainers to help schools make a successful transition to the new materials.

Notable Quote

"This is a way of looking at science education that many people in schools haven't been introduced to," said Claire Duggan, a leader of the IMPACT Center in Boston. "Making this change is something districts couldn't do on their own, which meant being ready to deal with teachers' issues, from providing model teaching of a unit to working through questions about selection and implementation."

Focusing on Issues of Rigor and Design

The process developed by EDC's K–12 Science Center to guide districts through curriculum selection and evaluation was broken into three stages, beginning with setting up a meaningful procedure for selecting curricula. In addition, EDC's K–12 Science Center encouraged the more than 500 isolated and underserved school districts it targeted to examine materials based on the key criteria of academic rigor, equity, and developmental appropriateness. *Academic rigor* focused on a curriculum's goals for learning, including building students' reasoning abilities, developing thinking particular to the subject area, and understanding methods for establishing and evaluating knowledge in the discipline. *Equity* meant looking at how well materials promoted high levels of achievement among a wide range of students by accommodating various learning styles and providing different kinds of opportunities for students to understand the subject-area content and demonstrate mastery. *Developmental appropriateness* examined how well curriculum materials were geared to the students they were designed to reach, with science content set at a level that built on students' prior knowledge and pushed toward deeper and more extensive understanding. EDC's K–12 Center asked districts it worked with to focus on six key questions. The first four questions are meant to reinforce the three criteria defined above, and the last two questions are about implementation:

1. How will the curriculum materials support the standards for teaching and learning? (Academic rigor)
2. How will educators create a coherent science program that has a deliberate and integrated design? (Academic rigor)
3. How will the curriculum materials both challenge and support students with diverse social and academic experiences to learn science successfully? (Equity)
4. How will the curriculum materials engage and motivate students to learn science successfully? (Developmental appropriateness)
5. What kind of professional development should the district provide that will enable teachers to implement standards-based curriculum materials effectively? (Implementation)
6. What implementation challenges do standards-based science curriculum materials present, and how do teachers and schools address them? (Implementation)

Finally, EDC's K–12 Center provided a curriculum evaluation tool that prompted curriculum reviewers to answer questions about the materials, providing specific evidence from the materials themselves to support their answers. Topics covered included instructional design, assessment, and alignment with standards. (See Appendix II for this tool.)

Breaking Down the Pedagogy

The LASER Center developed a different system for getting schools and districts to think about the rationale behind curriculum materials. The LASER Center's process drew from national science standards, the National Science Resources Center's (NSRC) previous reviews of science materials in connection with the National Academy of Sciences and the Smithsonian Institution, and its experience in schools. *Pedagogical appropriateness* encouraged selection teams to ask whether materials promoted effective science teaching and learning, emphasized inquiry and activity, and demonstrated developmental appropriateness. *Science content and presentation* focused on whether content in materials was accurate, up-to-date, and effectively presented, including checks of how well the materials connected to national science education standards. *Organization and format; materials, equipment, and supplies; and equity issues* covered topics such as the presentation of information, the clarity and adequacy of instructions for manipulating laboratory equipment, and the presence of appropriate safety precautions. Criteria addressing equity issues included asking whether the material was free of cultural, racial, gender, and age bias.

In this excerpt from its middle school–level evaluation guide, the LASER Center broke down the topic of "pedagogical appropriateness" into a battery of nine questions about inquiry and activity as the basis of learning experiences. For each question, the evaluation tool asked selection team members to answer yes or no and to elaborate with a short reason for their answer:

1. Does the material engage students in the processes of science?

2. Does the material engage students in planning and conducting scientific investigations?

3. Does the material provide opportunities for students to develop questioning skills related to scientific investigations?

4. Does the material provide opportunities for students to make and record their own observations?

5. Does the material provide opportunities for students to gather data and defend their own evidence?

6. Does the material provide opportunities, where appropriate, for students to use mathematics in the collection and treatment of data?

7. Does the material provide opportunities for students to express their results in a variety of ways?

8. Does the material encourage students to construct and analyze alternative explanations for science phenomena?

9. Does the material provide opportunities for students to work collaboratively with others?

Source: National Science Resources Center. (1998). *Evaluation Criteria for Middle School Science Curriculum Materials.*

Making Curriculum Selection an Inquiry Process

The SCI Center at BSCS developed an extensive process for helping select materials that it called the Analyzing Instructional Materials (AIM) process and tools. The process focused largely on research looking at how students learn science.

Using an inquiry-based approach to selection, AIM encouraged teams to ask questions, gather information, and make decisions about curriculum based on evidence. Rather than allowing teachers to take a cursory glance at the science content covered in a textbook, AIM encouraged teachers to think about the importance of curriculum materials in what students learn and how teachers teach. The AIM process involved teachers and administrators as a team. They completed a graphic organizer on the conceptual flow of content from a unit of instruction. Then, they used rubrics to analyze evidence from curriculum materials from four main areas: science content, the work students do, the work teachers do, and how student learning is assessed. Selection teams used scores from the four rubrics to compare curriculum materials and determine which options were most aligned with their criteria.

Because the collaborative AIM process required consensus building, it challenged teachers and science administrators to develop a common understanding about the curriculum materials under review. Most teachers came to the process of selecting materials hoping to find a textbook that covered the science content required by their district or state standards. The AIM process sought to help teachers also factor in the importance of the continuity and depth of reform-oriented curriculum materials, leading to a better understanding of standards-based approaches to learning and teaching science.

The process often raised questions about making the transition from seeing curriculum materials as a guide for what to teach to, for instance, how to teach science concepts in ways that are sensitive to various styles of learning. A structure that made time for reading, discussion, reflection, and working with a trained facilitator helped teachers and administrators work through such issues. The facilitator encouraged participants to base statements on evidence and suspend inferences until all evidence was shared. In the end, science teachers and administrators built a shared understanding of how well specific curriculum materials might meet the needs of their students. Along the way, participants also practiced gathering evidence to support their decisions. The design of the AIM process envisioned a transformative professional development experience where curriculum selection led participants to rethink basic issues about science, teaching, and learning.

Building the Foundation for a Successful Selection Process

Starting down the path to a new, more intensive curriculum requires a major local commitment to helping people understand, feel comfortable with, and ultimately master both a new way of teaching and a new vision of student learning.

A Selection Team Needs to Have the Right Players

The centers' experiences showed that teams should include individuals representing a variety of perspectives. Selection teams worked best when they included representatives from all schools affected by the process. In addition, both new and experienced teachers should be on the team, since each group offers a unique and important perspective on how curriculum materials can support teaching. Finally, special education staff and reading specialists can help the team consider whether the curriculum materials are accessible to all learners. District leaders in science or curriculum or the superintendent's office can also be helpful, particularly in dealing with longer-range implementation issues. "It was a tremendous growth opportunity for me as a central office administrator," said Tom Archer, science specialist for the Evergreen Public Schools in Vancouver, Washington, which was one of the districts that worked with the SCI Center on selection. "This was a way to get serious in thinking about what standards tell us we need to be doing, what works best for kids, and looking at evidence in making decisions instead of what we like or are used to."

Some Preparatory Work on Major Issues Helps Make Selection Meetings More Productive

Addressing basic issues—from research on learning or inquiry to beliefs about the role of curriculum materials in teaching—can be useful in developing common understandings ahead of the selection process. Preselection discussions can build awareness of available standards-based curriculum materials, how the national standards are embodied in the materials, and new inquiry-based teaching and assessment strategies. Some center leaders reported that team members were more likely to recognize standards-based teaching strategies in curriculum materials if they saw them modeled by facilitators and experienced the strategies from the learner's perspective.

Helping Selection Team Members Envision Themselves as Leaders Can Pay Dividends

Training in advance and the selection process itself can encourage team members to assume the role of curriculum leader and participate more actively in the systemic aspects of curriculum change. For example, having team members examine student work, achievement, and enrollment data as part of a larger assessment of the current science program can be a powerful experience that challenges the beliefs of team members and builds a shared vision of learning and teaching. A shared vision reduces the likelihood that members of the selection team will have opposing views on the characteristics of materials that best meet the needs of students. Seeing themselves as valuable contributors in a thoughtful selection process can help team members focus on the critical task of establishing the need for curricular change and advocating for such change throughout their work in schools or districts.

The Selection Process Can Be a Professional Learning Experience

Research has increasingly looked toward a selection process that is "educative"; that is, informing or educating participants as they do it. The work of the centers confirmed the value of making teachers key players in a collaborative process of aligning, selecting, and implementing curriculum materials.

In preparation for the first round of identifying curricula to consider for adoption, many districts routinely appoint a team composed of content-area coordinators and classroom teachers. The involvement of teachers, however, often ends once the curriculum materials are adopted and added to the approved district or state list. To maximize professional learning, centers found that teachers need to stay involved throughout the whole process—from establishing learning goals to implementing curriculum materials.

As teachers explore the standards, they learn that science is valued, collaborate with peers and experts, examine the extent to which assessments match content, reexamine their own classroom practices, work with others to solve problems, and interact with subject matter and pedagogy. All these activities enhance the professional growth of individual teachers and can lead to more effective teaching and learning practices.

Buy-in and Support Are Critical

The centers found various ways to encourage local buy-in: guarantees of release time for teachers, district matches for training costs, and getting school boards or parents to indicate their approval for the change in science education. Still, many of the districts that dropped out of the process between the time that they, for instance, visited regional offices to look at materials to the time of first-year training, or from the first year of training to the second, did so because of a lack of widespread support. Such occurrences led centers to encourage districts interested in the new materials to carefully consider teacher readiness and financial costs before committing to the selection and implementation process.

Frustrations and Failure Are Part of the Process

Helping educators make the selection process a more significant and thoughtful step in developing stronger science education programs led the four dissemination and implementation centers to recognize several key challenges in getting schools and districts to seriously consider a stronger, nontraditional curriculum. As a result, the centers drew lessons from the ways the process and their pitch for standards-based materials didn't work.

Not surprisingly, time and money were the main obstacles in getting local districts to opt for the more intensive selection process and the extensive professional development that came with implementation. Time and money were also the main reasons that teams dropped out of the process or did not follow through fully. Even after overcoming initial issues and assembling a strong selection team backed by outside help, some schools never realized the full potential of the new materials or withdrew from the process completely. Alternatively, districts involved with the centers saw some schools use the experience to overhaul classroom teaching and attitudes toward science, while other schools offered resistance to change. Even when education leaders saw value in the materials, many opted to stick with mainstream texts from familiar publishers or those that they thought would produce bigger short-term gains on achievement tests.

Awareness of Problems Led to Intervention

Knowing the challenges that could arise helped the center's staff members to know when they needed to intervene to quickly answer questions or erase confusion for local districts moving toward use of the standards-based materials. Pam Pelletier, who worked with the IMPACT Center, said that arranging for educators with questions about the materials to visit classrooms that were succeeding with high-quality materials often helped. Tom Williams of Mississippi College in Clinton, Mississippi, who led a regional hub as part of EDC's K–12 Center, said that success in helping schools was often the result of dedicated work. "Convincing districts to view new curricula as a serious option for their schools was a long and intensive process in many places, requiring many, many contacts with the hub," Williams stated.

Summary and Conclusion

Developing a curriculum selection process that emphasized the full scope of improved science education envisioned by the national standards was a cornerstone of the centers' mission. In so doing, the centers hoped to show schools and districts how to think more seriously about curriculum that engages students, deepens science knowledge, and advances the profession of science education.

The curriculum selection process championed by the centers was a far cry from the frequent status quo around the country, in which superficial impressions or a preference for familiar books or publishers bested other selection criteria. Instead, the centers advocated deep discussions among a wide variety of participants about expectations, teaching methods, standards, and achievement data—among other topics—as well as a systematic, evidence-based examination of curriculum materials. Rubrics applied to the study of the materials, the centers urged, could be customized locally but should always look at issues of design and rigor, including content, pedagogy, equity, and developmental appropriateness. Ideally, this would spur an evaluation of current practice and produce a common vision for new goals and strategies.

Curriculum materials selection can be structured in a way that serves schools and districts well beyond merely choosing materials. It can become an ongoing professional development experience that builds districtwide leadership capacity, deepens local learning communities, and expands the understanding of standards-based learning and teaching. The next chapter addresses those issues in more depth.

4

Professional Development for Curriculum Awareness, Adoption, and Implementation

Nancy M. Landes
Biological Sciences Curriculum Study

In many ways, the work of the four science dissemination and implementation centers amounted to a massive professional development blitz focused on bringing teachers up to speed on the inquiry-based science teaching and learning envisioned by national science standards. In the project, a focus on curriculum segued into a variety of work, delivered largely through professional development. In a more specific way, the centers supported the idea that the science curriculum that districts chose could anchor local professional development to upgrade the content, pedagogy, and assessment knowledge of teachers. In short, one of the centers' goals was to provide opportunities for teacher learning as rich and empowering as those that the new generation of instructional materials was designed to provide for students.

Although the centers defined professional development as opportunities for *teacher* learning, the audience for professional development often included school and district leaders in science education, university faculty, and community members, as well as practicing classroom science teachers. The centers sought an audience that corresponded with a basic belief that effective professional development for science reform encompasses learning for all those responsible for providing high-quality, standards-based science education to all students.

In many cases, the dissemination and implementation centers had to reinvent and redefine professional development for the educators involved in the work. Professional development for teachers often means a workshop or meeting lasting one day or less on a special topic or the development of a single skill, such as managing cooperative learning groups. When implementing new curriculum materials, teachers might be fortunate to experience a 2- to 3-hour session led by a representative of the curriculum's publisher who walks teachers through the materials and possibly provides an opportunity to try a lab or an activity from the curriculum. Many districts do not provide even that basic level of professional development as they adopt new instructional materials. Teachers are left to sink or swim based on their individual work or on the efforts of grade-level teams at elementary schools or in a science department in middle and high schools. Also rare is content-area professional development that complements the curriculum that teachers are using or that shows how the materials teachers use in class can be adapted to different student learning styles or combined with authentic assessment opportunities.

"[T]he professional development currently available to teachers is woefully inadequate," wrote Hilda Borko of the University of Colorado, Boulder, in 2004. "Each year, schools, districts, and the federal government spend millions, if not billions, of dollars on in-service seminars and other forms of professional development that are fragmented, intellectually superficial, and do not take into account what we know about how teachers learn." The dissemination and implementation centers took into account the available research on effective professional development and, to the extent possible, offered training that occurred over a longer time frame (months instead of days), was "job-embedded" (occurring as a part of the teachers' regular job and during regular hours), and was related directly to the daily work of teachers, focusing particularly on the knowledge and skills necessary for successful implementation of instructional materials. This level of depth marked a significant change from what most school districts and teachers had experienced previously.

Often through regional sites, the centers customized professional development for districts interested in adopting National Science Foundation (NSF)–supported materials and other standards-based materials. Services ranged from on-site consultation with school and district teams to summer institutes and online courses. Showcases and libraries of actual materials gave educators hands-on examples of the topics and methods in the curricula. Training helped district teams on topics from curriculum selection and planning to classroom implementation and helped create regional networks to expand opportunities for educators to learn from one another.

Building on Professional Development Research

The dissemination and implementation centers took great care in crafting professional development programs tied to curriculum. They began with the premise that teachers needed intensive, ongoing experiences if they were to change instructional practices and implement the standards-based instructional materials as intended. Each center used a different approach, but all four centers built their strategies around basic principles of effective professional development.

The Centers Saw the Instructional Materials as an Effective and Essential Centerpiece for the Professional Development of Teachers

In a project that aimed to show students how to learn science through skills such as observing and inferring, the centers saw professional development as a way to practice what they preached: Inquiry is central to science learning. When engaging in inquiry, students observe and explore objects and events, ask questions, construct explanations, test those explanations against current scientific knowledge, and describe and discuss their ideas and conclusions. They identify their assumptions, use critical and logical thinking, and consider alternative explanations. In this way, students actively develop their understanding of science by combining scientific knowledge with reasoning and thinking skills.

Joe Flynn, a senior project director at Education Development Center, Inc. (EDC), said the centers recognized that their job was to prepare the educators they worked with to not merely receive messages about professional development but also to explain what they learned about high-quality professional development to others. "The seminars offered by the [EDC] center included an introductory professional development experience about inquiry, emphasizing how inquiry learning differs from [so-called] hands-on science. The districts need to reinforce that distinction in all the professional development they do."

The IMPACT Center's cadre of professional development providers worked with teachers throughout New England in modeling lessons with students, engaging teachers in in-depth experiences with specific instructional materials, and providing ongoing support to teachers as they tried new inquiry-based practices in their classrooms. Modeling lessons also proved to be a strategy for dealing with teachers' diverse needs. Some elementary teachers, for example, needed to build their knowledge of content, while some high school colleagues were more focused on understanding new teaching techniques.

The Science Curriculum Implementation (SCI) Center in Colorado, meanwhile, engaged teachers in analyzing the instructional materials using tools to help them understand the "conceptual flow" of the lessons, chapters, or units of instruction. The SCI Center believed that by immersing teachers in examining how concepts were organized in the instructional materials, they deepened their content knowledge and could better focus on student learning as they taught. In this kind of training, teachers identified the big ideas and unifying themes that the materials developed over the course of the school year. Further, they considered how each lesson, chapter, and unit contributed to students' understanding of these ideas or themes. Teachers also determined how the sequence of learning experiences deepened student understanding over time. The center believed that when teachers understood how a well-designed unit of instruction provided coherent learning opportunities for their students, they were more likely to use the materials as designed. Or when teachers invariably adapted the materials to meet individual student or classroom needs, they could make those adaptations with an understanding of both the instructional model and conceptual flow of the materials and remain true to the philosophy of the curricular design.

The Centers Provided Opportunities for Teachers to Use the Materials From the Perspective of a Learner

The centers believed that teachers needed to have inquiry experiences if they were to become proficient teachers of inquiry-based science. Teachers were encouraged to complete actual learning experiences from the materials just as their students would. This was considered by the centers to be an important aspect of professional development because teachers often have trouble reaching students in the ways they learn best if the teachers themselves have not experienced that kind of learning. Such experiences also addressed the first impression some teachers had after looking at the materials: "My kids can't do this."

In workshops, EDC's K–12 Center staff members would have the teachers perform several science investigations taken straight from the materials, in addition to discussing the philosophy and pedagogy of the curriculum. The adult learners would start with the simpler activities and move to the more sophisticated ones, just as the students would progress through the materials—but compressed to fit the 90 minutes usually allotted for a workshop. For example, in "Circuits and Pathways," a module for Grades 4 and 5 from EDC-developed *Insights: An Inquiry-Based Elementary School Science Curriculum*, the teachers would be given a battery, a wire, and a bulb and asked to get the bulb to light up. They would then be asked, just as the students would, to draw on paper the ways that they tried to do that, including both the successful attempts and the unsuccessful ones.

The Centers Invited Administrators to Share in the Vision

The centers' work also involved district leaders in creating this vision of effective classroom learning and teaching in science. For instance, EDC's K–12 Center made a point of inviting superintendents in the rural and underserved districts it targeted to be involved in its professional development.

Tom Williams, the chairman of the teacher education and leadership department at Mississippi College and an advisor in a regional hub of EDC's K–12 Center, explained how the center sought to involve district administrators: "We had dinner for superintendents to hit it from the top," he said. "We asked them how they saw science education playing a part in their district. We wanted them to talk to us about how they saw science education. We let them talk and we listened."

Williams's hub in Mississippi used a different strategy for building principals' buy-in. "With principals, we had a breakout room with kids," he recalled. "We brought in the materials from the local schools, such as the physics kit. We provided principals a model lesson so they could see what the lesson would look like in their school."

Such carefully choreographed introductions to the centers' professional development for district administrators and principals helped build the vision of what science education should look like in a district's classrooms and build support for the implementation of high-quality curricula.

The Centers Used Training as a First Step in Creating Long-Term Communities of Practice Where Teachers Could Learn From Each Other

In Delaware, the LASER Center built a learning community among a statewide coalition of science educators through its leadership institutes, said Jack Collette, senior consultant with the Delaware Foundation for Science and Mathematics Education. Four Delaware teams representing seven school districts attended a National Science Resources Center (NSRC) leadership institute on elementary science education reform that proved to be a catalytic event. The groups coalesced into a single dynamic team that committed to work together on a 5-year plan to implement a kit-based science curriculum in their districts. The group included teachers, curriculum supervisors, administrators, representatives from businesses and the University of Delaware, and a science expert from the state department of education who had led the standards development process.

The pilot program, designed to provide 360 teachers in the seven districts (approximately one third of the state's K–6 teachers) with one science kit and the necessary professional development, proved popular with teachers, students, and parents. The professional development offered a new level of depth and intensity in training for elementary teachers, with a group of teachers meeting with a master science teacher for a total of 30 hours over an 8- to 10-week period. The teachers worked through each lesson in a given science unit, learning both the science content and the inquiry pedagogy. This experience was a world apart from the typical "make-and-take" evening or half-day workshops many were used to attending. The program garnered praise from the state board of education, and there was a strong demand to introduce additional kits the following year and offer the program to more teachers.

The development of arrangements in which teachers could work together over a long period of time was an important part of such a process, said Jeff Estes, manager of science and engineering education for the Pacific Northwest National Laboratory in Richland, Washington, who worked with a regional LASER Center. "It's a difficult step for teachers to discard what they believe for what the knowledge base says," he noted.

The Centers' Training Prepared Teachers to Take On Leadership Roles

In curriculum-based professional development, teachers often emerge as leaders in supporting their colleagues through the implementation of new curriculum materials. Those teachers will then act as agents of change in the school or district and help to sustain the curriculum reform effort. They might become mentors for new teachers or resource teachers in a department or at a grade level. Encouraging teachers who show an interest in taking a leadership role can be especially effective if their work comes with release time that allows them to help in other teachers' classrooms.

The Boston public schools participated in the SCI Center's professional development on reform at the high school level. The district assembled a team of six high school teacher leaders, a medical school faculty member, and two professional development specialists to attend the SCI Center's National Academy for Curriculum Leadership for three summers. "This academy helped our teacher leaders to understand how to select curriculum more effectively, how to design professional development, and how to evaluate professional development," said Marilyn Decker, the senior program director for science in the Boston public schools. Once back in the district, the team led in the selection and implementation of new biology and chemistry curricula.

In addition, the Boston schools have adopted lessons learned through IMPACT training, said Ms. Decker, a former leader of the IMPACT Center. "Today, all kits and curriculum-based professional development is designed and delivered by teachers [trained by

IMPACT consultants]," she said. "Our teacher leaders now coteach (with university professors) university content courses that are aligned with our curriculum. This year, the teacher leader instructional team will deliver over 50,000 hours of professional development."

The Centers Looked at Ways to Assess the Effectiveness of Their Professional Development

Each of the centers agreed that professional development that is focused on curriculum can and should be readily assessed.

1. Are teachers actually implementing the curriculum as designed?

2. Has the professional development experience resulted in changes in teachers' attitudes and collaboration with others?

3. Is the curriculum implementation resulting in higher student achievement?

4. Are the goals of the professional development experiences being achieved, and if not, what modifications in future professional development might be required?

These and other questions can help schools and districts assess the quality and impact of teacher professional development experiences and consider creating longer-term, job-embedded opportunities rather than short-term, isolated ones.

Addressing Professional Development Challenges

Fulfilling the demands of building myriad professional development structures to help educators, administrators, and even community leaders to develop the skills and confidence needed to implement the standards-based materials provided many challenges. The four dissemination and implementation centers sometimes had to adapt their plans to the realities of participants' needs. However, such planning and refining helped the centers improve their efforts to help schools and districts consider and adopt exemplary curriculum materials and see how they could be a catalyst for improving professional development.

Meeting Participants' Varying Needs Can Be a Challenge in a Process That Seeks Wide Involvement and Collaboration

Audiences for professional development represented different levels of schooling, different roles within education, different levels of understanding of (or interest in) the issues involved, as well as different schools, districts, and even states. In some cases, the audience included college-level education faculty, employees of private-sector science companies, or members of the community. These differences might have occurred within a single district team or across an audience at a summer institute. Delivering messages that made sense to a diverse audience created an immediate challenge for the centers in designing the content of professional development. Training needed to be accompanied by follow-up help for those needing it, not only within the learning opportunities the centers provided but also in school settings as participants used what they had learned—a challenge for both the center's trainers and for the participants.

Winning Local Educators' Involvement Requires an Awareness of Prevailing Notions Toward Nontraditional Materials

One big challenge in getting schools and districts on board and holding their interest was countering inaccurate notions that inquiry-based teaching is, among other things, a progressive fad that abandons teaching "the basics." Professional development that helped participants understand the materials and broaden acceptance in their schools and communities often came with advice on how to explain the materials and acquaint people with the goals of the national science standards in a way that made immediate sense and showed everyday applications or benefits for going the more challenging route on teaching and assessment.

Training Needs to Be Structured to Move Participants Toward a Mastery Level

Centers began with the goal of making schools and teachers users of the standards-based instructional materials. With that goal, one regional center leader said that most of the professional development work concentrated on moving educators from not using inquiry-based curriculum at all to at least a basic or "mechanical" level of usage. Because of practical constraints and the duration of the work, less center training was devoted to moving educators to an expert level. Although some schools and districts developed their own systems for building expertise from within, the centers did not have the means to devote a large portion of their resources to helping teachers really master pedagogy or assessment concepts built into the inquiry materials. On the other hand, centers did help schools and districts think through long-range issues such as the steps involved in sustaining the commitment to inquiry-based materials and increasing teachers' "fidelity" to understanding and covering the curriculum in a way that was true to its design.

Training Focused on Curriculum Issues Is Helpful, but a Long-Term Strategy Is Needed to Address Shortcomings in Teacher Preparation

While the centers' professional development work was designed to work within the confines of the NSF-funded program, one center leader said that the training showed the need for colleges of education and state education departments to improve training requirements for teachers to learn about inquiry-oriented teaching and assessment and how to make classrooms more focused on active student learning and collaborative investigations.

The centers' work spun off some results in that area. University partners in EDC's K–12 Center's work in South Dakota, for example, turned work with schools on science curriculum into new aspects of college-level training for educators. Hub leaders succeeded in 2005 in establishing a K–12 Science Education Specialist credential in that state, which was directly influenced by its work with EDC's K–12 Center. Black Hills State University (BHSU) also developed the coursework required to earn the specialist designation for both those teachers working within a master's degree program and those seeking certification after obtaining their master's. In addition, K–8 science kits used as part of the hub's curriculum library are also used in BHSU's teacher education programs.

Meanwhile, Joe Bellina, a professor of physics at Saint Mary's College in Notre Dame, Indiana, who worked with EDC's K–12 Center's northern Indiana hub, reported to EDC staff members in 2006: "We have fundamentally changed the way in which Saint Mary's College helps its elementary education majors learn science. . . . We have been able to create a two-semester course in physical science which functions as a laboratory for the education courses that can only describe best practice. In our classroom, we model it."

A Letter from South Carolina: The Ups and Downs of Transforming Professional Development

Tom Peters, the director of South Carolina's Coalition for Mathematics and Science, located at Clemson University, wrote down his thoughts in December 2006 about the work of the LASER Center in South Carolina. His words appear below, with only minor editing:

The Successes

As we became involved with LASER, we were already four years into an NSF Statewide Systemic Initiative that established 13 regional professional development "hubs" across our state. This meant we had an infrastructure of people and places from which to deliver PD [professional development], and we had money to buy down the cost of kits and training for schools and districts to try them out. Once most of our hub community got on board with the idea of promoting kit-based science, we could deliver massive amounts of basic training to move elementary and, eventually, middle-grades teachers from using texts toward using inquiry-based materials.

This people infrastructure also made it easier to offer Strategic Planning Institutes (SPIs), as we did not need to bring in lots of folks from other places to deliver the program. We did three SPIs in South Carolina during the LASER years. We also looked at the South Carolina institutes and others offered nationally and in other LASER states as a professional development opportunity for our hub science and math specialists. So, involvement in delivery of LASER events sharpened and expanded our skill base as PD providers.

When things worked well, we'd have school districts participate in an SPI and they'd go home to the support of their local hub for professional development and, sometimes, materials support, too.

Following our science instructional materials adoption in 2000–2001, I estimated that [about] 80% of all elementary schools in South Carolina were using at least some inquiry-based instructional materials for science. We also had some helpful assistance from our state, which wisely invested in ongoing funding of refurbishments for inquiry-based materials!

There is no doubt in my mind that all this "sodbusting" changed the landscape of science education in South Carolina. Expectations have risen for having instructional time for elementary science and for what good instruction looks like in all science. Not surprisingly, we led the nation in improvement on NAEP in grade 4 science. Our grade 8 improvement wasn't bad, either.

The Challenges

If you look carefully at the dates above, you'll see one of our more vexing challenges. Our science instructional materials adoption was in 2000–2001. Most of our work with SPIs took place after that. Had we been able to do SPIs as a precursor

(Continued)

(Continued)

to the state's adoption cycle, I think we'd have had a more powerful impact. Districts would have created proactive implementation plans instead of reactive ("I've got all these kits, what do I do now?") plans. Why were we behind the curve? Mostly it had to do with generating [the money] needed to get teams to participate in the SPI; $5,000 a team was a great [amount] of money for poor South Carolina school districts. It took us a few years to develop the corporate partnerships we needed to get South Carolina LASER off the ground and make SPIs affordable.

We were also challenged by our success at the basics. Just managing introductory kit training was a heavy load for the hubs. Every year would bring new teachers, grade-level switches, and, sometimes, new kits due to changes in our state science standards. We collectively insisted on professional development as a precursor to receiving kits: a good idea—and a monster to manage.

We were challenged by 9/11 and by the end to the Eisenhower [professional development] program.... Both hit our school district partners hard financially, making funds that had been available for science PD very scarce. These, combined with changing directions in our Statewide Systemic Initiative, made it harder for us to maintain the rigor and relevance of PD associated with getting schools to implement inquiry-based materials with fidelity.

We were also challenged by a lack of similar materials in mathematics. This might sound weird, but it's true. As a science and math systemic initiative, we were challenged to keep our math community engaged with LASER, because there weren't quite the same choices in inquiry-based mathematics materials.... SPIs being science only [was] off-putting to some members of our math community and to some school districts, as well. We ended up addressing the math issue head-on by developing an inquiry-based math curriculum, *Math Out of the Box*, in partnership with Clemson University [published by Carolina Biological Supply Company], and by recasting the SPI as a science and math institute. This broadening of focus brought the LASER era to a close in South Carolina.

Source: South Carolina's Coalition for Mathematics and Science. "Re: A quick question," December 21, 2006 (to Lonnie Harp). Used by permission.

Summary and Conclusion

The four science centers advocated that once a science curriculum had been selected, it could anchor local professional development to upgrade content, pedagogy, and assessment knowledge of teachers. Generally, the centers ran professional development that involved providing teachers with a better understanding of inquiry and offered both in-depth learning experiences with specific instructional materials and ongoing support to teachers as they began to use the materials in their classrooms. The centers operated under the assumption that the better the teachers understood the design of the materials—and the reasons for that design—the more likely they were to use the materials as intended. But centers included administrators, too, because of the belief that truly effective professional development involves all of the players providing or overseeing science education.

Persuading teachers and administrators that both parties had to work together, however, often meant re-creating the vision participants had in their minds of what constitutes effective professional development. The centers' work was not conducted in the mold so frequently seen: a superficial 2- to 3-hour workshop that does not relate to what teachers are doing in their classrooms on a daily basis. Instead, based on research into effective professional development, the centers offered customized trainings over a longer time frame (days, weeks, or even months) that focused on helping teachers understand and successfully use curriculum materials with their students.

The centers' experiences with professional development revealed several paths that can lead to lasting change. Creating communities of practice in which teachers can learn from one another is an important way to help teachers embrace a new curriculum and/or instructional approach. Preparing teachers to assume leadership roles creates a cadre of people who not only can implement reforms but can help sustain them into the future as well. Finally, exposing institutions of higher education to innovative professional development can lead to changes in teacher preparation programs, as occurred in both Indiana and South Dakota.

5

The Role of Assessments and Accountability

Sally Goetz Shuler, Judi Backman, and Steve Olson
National Science Resources Center

The curriculum materials developed through the National Science Foundation's (NSF) Instructional Materials Development program may offer the clearest illustration of the difference between textbook-driven science classrooms and the new system of science education envisioned by the *National Science Education Standards*. The innovative materials sought to reinvent science teaching and learning as a series of engaging investigations focused on real-life problems, hands-on activities, and a greater understanding of the big concepts that unite science facts. The learning activities were filled with continual opportunities for teachers to assess students' skills and progress. They did so in ways that blended active teaching focused on inquiry and assessments built around challenges similar to those faced by real-life scientists.

Here are some examples of assessments from standards-based curricula:

- In the introductory assessment of a K–1 curriculum module on life science, a teacher is given criteria for evaluating students' first drawings of a plant. Students include in their drawings all of the things a plant needs to grow and whether they can smell or hear those things.
- Middle school students studying space science keep logs of the phases of the moon for a month and learn to distinguish one phase from the other. Then, they must show the teacher they can simulate the phases using models of the moon, Earth, and sun. An observation checklist permits the teacher to note each student's understanding of the moon's four primary phases.
- While studying semiconductors, high school students participate in a team challenge that involves building and testing a robot. Teachers, watching the students' work and performance, judge students' accomplishments along several dimensions: following protocols, describing components involved in their work, discussing their project as a team, making modifications after testing, and more.

These activities and assessment opportunities include typical features of the new generation of research- and standards-based curriculum materials, such as student drawings and performances and teacher observations. As the dissemination and implementation centers funded by the NSF worked to gain exposure and acceptance for the new materials, they promoted a critical message: The curriculum used by teachers in classrooms should lead to new thinking about assessment, as well as about the ways teaching and gauging student progress can combine to provide meaningful learning experiences for both teachers and students.

Beyond the challenge of introducing new modes of classroom assessment, developments in large-scale state assessments and the adoption of state science standards across the country also complicated the work of implementing new curriculum materials. In important ways, *both* the promise and the challenge of the centers' work on assessment grew from the same source as the curriculum project itself: the setting of science standards.

Notable Quote

Ensuring that their messages about assessment were understood was a key task for the centers, and it posed a problem. "District leaders were much more

> concerned with the challenges of managing kit-based materials, developing efficient materials-management systems, and organizing adequate teacher professional development," said Sally Goetz Shuler, executive director of the National Science Resources Center in Washington, D.C. "Districts often found those tasks overwhelming. Only when they overcame those kinds of concerns did they begin to examine deficits in students' content knowledge and become more interested in assessment."

Supporting New Frontiers in Classroom Assessment

The goal of the national science standards went well beyond defining what students should know and be able to do. The standards called for a new approach to all facets of science education. "To attain the vision of science education described in the Standards, change is needed in the entire system" was the approach explained in the standards chapter devoted to improvements in science teaching. The first expectation in that chapter—identified as Standard A—was that teachers would "plan an inquiry-based science program for their students." Hand in hand with changes in pedagogy were changes in classroom assessment to complement the inquiry emphasis. A full chapter in the science standards was devoted to assessment, explaining, in detail, ways of assessing students' abilities to inquire and their understanding of the natural world. In both areas, the standards pointed toward new options for students and teachers. Summary discussions, student journals, performance events, data analysis tasks, and scenarios where students designed experiments were seen as key classroom activities that would offer feedback to teachers, students, and parents on students' mastery of a range of science concepts and abilities. As the standards document stated, "Assessment practices and policies provide operational definitions of what is important. For example, the use of an extended inquiry for an assessment task signals what students are to learn, how teachers are to teach, and where resources are to be allocated."

Developers of the standards-based instructional materials captured the new teaching and assessment directions in their materials, embedding activities that could provide important assessment feedback in routine lessons and incorporating more group projects and research that would lead students to performance events in which they could demonstrate their skills, knowledge, and ability to communicate on real science tasks.

A major difficulty facing all four centers involved preparing teachers and administrators to be able to understand and use the new kinds of assessments built into the materials. Most teachers lacked a view of assessment informed by the kind of teaching and learning research that informed the standards and the materials supported by the NSF and others. Finding the time and right experiences to build local educators' capacity for assessment proved time-consuming. In addition, administrative support was needed for large groups of teachers to make the transition.

On the positive side, however, the centers had several points of leverage in helping school systems improve science assessments, including the fact that because of their close association with curriculum developers, they were in a unique position to demonstrate to educators what promising new assessments looked like.

The four dissemination and implementation centers used many strategies to build new knowledge and capacity for classroom assessment. Some of the more frequently used tactics are highlighted below.

The Centers Acquainted Local Teams With the Assessment Concepts and Techniques Built Into the Standards-Based Curricula

The Science Curriculum Implementation (SCI) Center used a 5-day summer institute to introduce teams of two teachers and a key administrator to evaluating and selecting curricula, in part through the use of rubrics that identified good assessments within well-crafted curricula. During the school year after the summer institute, each team focused on helping teachers to use those curricula back in their home schools. A prominent emphasis was the use of formative assessments, which can record student knowledge before or during instruction, to drive both teaching and learning. (Perhaps more familiar are summative assessments, which evaluate achievement at the end of instruction.) Teachers examined student work to try to understand student thinking. Teachers also were taught to assess their own educational beliefs and pedagogical practices and then were provided with the tools and resources to bring those beliefs and practices into line with inquiry-based materials.

EDC's K–12 Center, meanwhile, held regional seminars to identify assessment issues and opportunities related to implementing the assessments presented in standards-based curricula. The introductory sessions were intended to give teams interested in the standards-based instructional materials the basic knowledge they would need to start working on assessment issues included in the curricula. Participant responses at a second-year seminar revealed that teachers were still trying to get a handle on the basics of the new assessment techniques. This discovery led EDC's K–12 Center staff members to alter their plan. Instead of delving deeper into helping teachers work through assessment issues, they developed tools that would help educators better understand assessment methods that support inquiry-based classrooms. "In a sense, it seemed like too much, too fast," said Karen Worth, a senior research scientist at EDC who helped design the center's work with its regional hubs and local educators on assessment. "Focusing more on the different kinds of assessment that exist and different ways of looking at them seemed like it would be more useful. Given where people were, that may have been the better way to go in the first place."

The Centers Provided Curriculum Experts to Model Teaching and Assessment Strategies in Schools and Districts Using the Exemplary Materials

The centers responded to the needs of schools by offering on-the-spot demonstrations of how the instructional materials worked in concert with the embedded assessments to create a classroom where inquiry was practiced even as it was taught. The IMPACT Center, like other centers, focused on assessment issues within the context of the larger teaching and learning goals of the standards-based curricula. The center's assistance team, which included a corps of implementation advisors who shepherded specific districts or schools through the process of selection and use, and a separate network of curriculum trainers focused on assessment as a key part of making the instructional materials work. Curriculum trainers who modeled lessons for teachers or worked on specific issues would consult with teachers on analyzing student work or showing how various assessment strategies might work in practice. The center found that although its assistance was useful and needed in the New England districts where it worked—and helped the schools involved truly implement the curriculum—it also exposed the need for teachers at all experience levels to have a greater understanding of how to conceptualize and use new types of assessments, such as those included in the materials.

> **Notable Quote**
>
> Informing teachers about new teaching and assessment techniques, building their comfort levels and leadership capacity, and helping them to successfully implement new strategies is a major undertaking, said Kim Bess, director of science for the San Diego City Schools, who worked with the SCI Center. "We're asking teachers to use curriculum materials that require them to release center stage to kids, organize students in work groups, and keep track of how they learn and what they know. You have to be ready for people to agree with you in meetings and then go into the classroom, feel frustrated, and just ask for a list of questions they should ask kids. This is an area where many of our teachers have had no personal experience, no training, and they probably like a lot of what they're already doing."

The Centers Created New Tools to Explain Assessment Strategies

EDC's K–12 Center created "Evidence of Understanding: An Introduction to Assessments in K–12 Science Curricula," a Web-based resource that acquaints users with more than 50 examples of assessments from exemplary science instructional materials. The types of assessments—which span the earth, physical, and life sciences and the elementary, middle, and high school levels—include observational assessments, written assessments, performance assessments, graphic assessments, and reflective self-assessments. The tool offers educators an opportunity to see many types of assessments from a variety of currently available instructional materials. The Web guide also shows how the materials' different types of assessments help students develop the skills needed to be successful on state accountability tests. The guide provides examples of questions taken from the released items of state exams and national standardized tests.

EDC's K–12 Center also developed two online courses on assessment for middle school educators. Each six-session course (30 hours over 8 weeks) was designed for teachers who want to understand more about national and state science tests and how these assessments can be incorporated into science units. Each course analyzed written, open-ended, multiple-choice, graphic, and performance assessments. As part of the course, participants could try out sample tasks with their students, share student work, and contribute ideas and understandings online. Later, EDC's K–12 Center used the online course and resource materials to conduct assessment workshops and presentations at national and regional meetings and conferences of the National Science Teachers Association.

As the Centers Pushed Educators to Try New Assessment Practices, the Educators Tried to Stick With the Familiar

Many of the challenges that shaped the assessment-related work of centers involved building the capacity in schools and districts to see beyond the entrenched demands of teaching cut-and-dried science content for quick-answer tests. Finding sufficient time to help teachers and district leaders become comfortable with new assessment practices was a constant hurdle. Some teachers implemented research-based curricula but continued to use tests and assessments from previous materials, partly because they were more familiar with the older assessments and did not feel ready to make the transition to new forms.

The centers found that many districts tended to ignore formative assessment in the initial stages of implementation, said Barbara Brauner Berns, then codirector of EDC's K–12 Center. Other center leaders agreed that the time and resources required for building teachers' capacity for understanding innovative, classroom-based assessment are extensive. Kim Bess, director of science for the San Diego City Schools, who worked with the SCI Center on implementing inquiry materials in high schools and middle schools, summed up those challenges this way: "You have to realize that, as teachers are struggling with issues of formative versus summative assessment, they still have to give out a report card at the end of the semester."

Navigating the Straits of Accountability Testing

The national science education standards led developers of the NSF-supported materials and other standards-based materials to new designs for teaching and learning that included inquiry-based curricula and more active and collaborative forms of assessment. In wider education circles, however, the chief legacy of the standards was their definition of what all students should know and be able to do. The content standards shaped the work of state standards panels. In turn, state standards influenced the science assessments developed in many states. By the end of the 1990s, almost all states had instituted uniform statewide tests designed, at least in part, to help drive changes in curriculum and improve teaching and learning. However, those large-scale, often high-stakes tests usually adapted the content statements of academic standards into traditional forms of standardized testing—more closely aligned with the structure and content of traditional textbooks than the learning objectives of the research-based curricula.

During the life of the dissemination and implementation centers, President George W. Bush signed into law the No Child Left Behind Act of 2001, which increased the pressure on schools to institute accountability testing and to craft responses to the results. The potential for synergy—and for conflict—between large-scale tests and the more cutting-edge assessments built into research-based curricula ultimately became a major consideration for all of the dissemination and implementation centers.

Problem solving, critical thinking, and creativity tend to be slighted on large-scale tests in favor of recalling facts and performing procedures—the kinds of rote tasks the national science standards sought to change. State assessments are often the centerpiece of accountability systems used to judge schools—and, sometimes, the performance of teachers and students. Being such a powerful force, large-scale assessments proved to be an effective driver of local decisions about curriculum materials and assessments. A common challenge for the centers was responding to the pressure that schools and districts felt to focus classroom time on preparation for large-scale tests, while overlooking the need for, say, formative assessments. School systems were sometimes hard-pressed to see how a cutting-edge curriculum conformed to a larger educational system in which students and schools were evaluated in ways that assume traditional—not innovative—teaching and learning approaches. The centers' staff members had to learn how to make a tough sell, doing so in part by broadening educators' attention from a single-minded focus on state test performance to the root goal of the national science standards: stimulating deeper student learning experiences in science classrooms.

Each of the dissemination and implementation centers dealt in its own way with the extent to which large-scale assessment influenced local districts and schools in evaluating or using the standards-based materials. Common strategies in helping educators work through the issues raised by the pressure of state assessment and accountability systems are highlighted below, with examples of specific work from individual centers.

The Centers Aligned Local Use of the Cutting-Edge Instructional Materials With State Standards and Assessment Systems

In establishing relationships with those responsible for the form and content of state assessments, the LASER Center found different situations in states across the country. In some states, the lack of alignment between research-based curricula and state assessments created a barrier to promoting exemplary instructional materials. In other states, changes in state science standards and assessments helped drive reform in science education toward a vision in line with the NSF-funded work.

In Delaware and Washington State, for instance, the LASER staff members worked with state officials to modify state assessment systems to better reflect the kind of science education offered through the research-based curricula. The alignment of large-scale assessments with the state standards and new curricula produced some promising initial results. In Delaware, where elementary school science programs are now based almost entirely on research-based instructional materials developed by LASER's parent, NSRC, 87% of students at the end of third grade and 70% of students at the end of fifth grade met or exceeded the state's performance standards for science. The year before the new materials were adopted, about 63% met the state's goals.

More recently, on the 2005 administration of the National Assessment of Educational Progress (NAEP) in science, South Carolina, another LASER site, showed the greatest gains of any of 44 participating states in the scores of its fourth graders, compared with the results in 2000. Similarly, South Carolina's eighth graders showed the nation's third-best improvement in scores. The gains came across the board—including among low-income students, African American students, and those with disabilities. South Carolina was one of only five states (along with California, Hawaii, Kentucky, and Virginia) to show improvement in both grades tested on the 2005 NAEP.

The centers also took advantage of initiatives within school systems to influence changes in state standards, curriculum frameworks, instructional materials, assessments, and/or professional development. By maintaining control of the connections among these parts of a state's science education system, the centers could help unite disparate school-improvement efforts. Thus changes in any part of the system became part of more comprehensive efforts to change the system as a whole.

"In our work with districts, part of our alignment of instructional materials with the state standards identified topics or areas where a greater emphasis was needed or different information might be needed to fill a gap in covering what the state was expecting," said Jeff Estes, a regional LASER leader in Washington State. "We also tried to help schools think about what to do, since the way the [state] assessment was constructed didn't match up with what the curriculum was leading to, [thereby confronting] the pressure to go with paper-and-pencil or multiple-choice or short-answer questions that would be what students would be seeing on the state test."

The Centers Used the Spotlight on Assessment and Accountability to Move Educators Toward a Greater Focus on Using Data to Make Decisions

At its regional hubs, EDC's K–12 Center offered training through the "Using Data" workshops, an initiative funded by the NSF. The program helped educators to understand educational data and to practice using multiple measures and levels of data to evaluate findings and make decisions. Nancy Love, the former director of the project for TERC in Cambridge, Massachusetts (now with Research for Better Teaching, Inc.), and a coauthor of *The Data Coach's Guide to Improving Learning for All Students,* said the process guides educators toward finding meaningful ways to use data from assessments of all kinds. "Data teams investigate not scientific phenomena or mathematics problems but how to improve teaching and learning. They raise questions, examine student learning and other data, test their hypotheses and share findings with their colleagues." The training highlighted how analyzing school performance data was an adult application of the kind of inquiry that was the aim of exemplary science teaching. In addition, the SCI Center used the process with teams to practice using available data to foster dialogue and change by identifying achievement gaps and other achievement issues, and it emphasized how data analysis provides a way for large-scale assessments and formative assessments to be used together to realize a common goal: improved student achievement.

South Dakota's exposure to such a program might not have happened were it not for EDC's K–12 Center, said Ben Sayler, director of the Center for the Advancement of Mathematics and Science Education at Black Hills State University in Spearfish, South Dakota. "We learned of Nancy Love's 'Using Data' process and were inspired to bring it to South Dakota entirely due to our participation as a hub," he said.

Summary and Conclusion

Alongside the centers' aim to gain exposure and acceptance for the standards-based instructional materials was the companion goal of transforming assessment so that it meshed with the new materials and enhanced teachers' abilities to measure student learning. It turned out, though, that the centers frequently had to retool their original plans for professional development for teachers around assessment because they discovered that educators needed more than a cursory introduction to how the assessment methods complemented standards-based curricula. Despite the centers' best efforts, it often seemed as if more time should be devoted to the assistance and professional development they offered; teachers had a tendency to want to stick with familiar assessment methods, even as they used the new curriculum materials.

The work of the centers highlighted not only the need to have strategies for bringing teachers, schools, and districts on board with innovative assessments but also the need for tactics addressing the ways that state and national assessments and accountability programs affect attitudes and actions in schools. The centers dealt with this reality head-on by looking for ways to work with leaders at the state level to align state assessments with the new, exemplary instructional materials and by assisting local educators on how to marry the demands of state tests with the types of instruction and assessment encouraged by the curricula.

Those seeking to improve preK–12 science education will likely have to contend with continually changing public-policy climates, both locally and nationally, but the use of large-scale, high-stakes tests seems established. It remains a big factor to consider for any school system touting more individualized and creative forms of classroom assessment.

6

Lessons Learned From Evaluation

Katrina Laguarda
Policy Studies Associates, Inc.

The preceding chapters of this book have told the story of what happened when the four science dissemination and implementation centers encouraged schools, districts, and states to consider and use standards-based instructional materials in science. However, it is important to note that the centers' work was always intended as an experiment, with a clear focus on understanding and sharing the lessons learned, regardless of the level of success. It is in that spirit that the authors present this chapter.

This chapter offers a summary of the results of six external evaluation activities: the four studies of project implementation and outcomes that each center commissioned from outside evaluators, the National Science Foundation (NSF)–commissioned cross-site program evaluation, and the analytic paper that examined dissemination and implementation center design options, which was also commissioned by the NSF. The authors hope the evaluation findings presented here provide some additional context for the concluding chapter's advice for those interested in taking up the cause championed by the centers.

Different Strategies, Different Settings

Over the course of approximately 5 years, the centers amassed a wealth of experience and insight through their work. They used different strategies to tackle the challenge of disseminating and implementing a new science curriculum, but despite those different strategies, they shared a common vision of the type of work necessary to realize the goal of getting exemplary curriculum materials in place in more U.S. classrooms. All four centers developed a menu of training, tools, and consultation that they delivered to district teams. One center, IMPACT New England, also trained and certified a cadre of 300 curriculum trainers, often classroom teachers, who could introduce schools and districts to new curriculum materials and prepare teachers to use them.

Three of the four centers—EDC's K–12 Center, the LASER Center, and the IMPACT Center—worked with a large number of districts through a network of regional satellites, housed at colleges, universities, and science organizations sponsored by states or federally funded programs. The remaining center, the SCI Center at the Biological Sciences Curriculum Study (BSCS), worked intensively with a relatively small number of district teams (25 in total, representing 19 districts). The regional satellites typically received modest grants from the centers to underwrite their work.

The three centers varied in the extent to which they relied on regional satellites to carry out their work with districts. For example, the IMPACT regional satellites assumed primary responsibility for helping districts to assess their science program needs, select and implement appropriate curricula, and support teacher professional development. The IMPACT Center staff supported regional centers by running retreats for regional leadership teams, consulting with regional center staff, training and certifying curriculum trainers, and establishing a Web site for information dissemination. The center did not work directly with districts in the regions they served. By contrast, EDC's K–12 Center and the LASER Center assumed primary responsibility for designing and delivering their core series of seminars to districts in the regions served by these centers. Their regional satellites played a supporting role in these activities, providing logistical support for regional meetings (renting space, catering meals, and transporting materials) and assisting in recruiting districts for seminars. Regional satellites also provided some follow-up to districts after they had attended institutes, hosted district teams at curriculum libraries, facilitated curriculum adoption committees, or answered questions. Because establishing these networks and building their capacity to support the adoption of new curriculum materials was a central part of the work of these three centers, at least two of the project evaluations focused primarily on the evolution of the regional satellites and the progress made by the dissemination centers in building their capacity.

At the local level, all four centers targeted services to district teams that were meant to assume responsibility for curriculum leadership. The centers adopted various strategies for recruiting and selecting district teams. District teams always included teachers from a variety of science disciplines and grade levels. Indeed, across all four centers, the majority of participants in dissemination center training and other activities were teachers. In addition, centers requested that district teams include at least one administrator—often an assistant superintendent or a science curriculum coordinator—who could advocate effectively for science reform and curriculum adoption. In some cases, district teams also included school principals. According to evaluations, the centers paid careful attention to the composition and recruitment of district teams. However, both the IMPACT Center and EDC's K–12 Center found that teams from rural districts had more difficulty attending institutes and other center activities because of both distance and the lack of staff to cover classes or district business. For example, two high school science teachers attending a center event on behalf of a small school might have composed the entire science department. EDC's K–12 Center relaxed its requirements for district team membership midway through the project, allowing smaller teams of teachers (with or without a district administrator) to attend seminars, increasing district participation in project activities as a result.

Building Demand, Offering Help

All four centers trained educators to review, evaluate, and select a curriculum appropriate for their students' and schools' needs. In addition to leading districts through the adoption process, the centers provided training and planning to help school systems create an infrastructure to support successful implementation of new curricula: teacher and administrator buy-in, teacher professional development, materials support, K–12 alignment, modes of assessment that fit with inquiry-based materials, and community support, among other issues. Given a broad mission and limited resources, the centers had to choose between activities designed to create demand for research-based materials and activities designed to support districts that had already decided to adopt such materials. At one end of the continuum, EDC's K–12 Center invested heavily in planning institutes and other activities designed to introduce districts to reform-oriented science education and research-based materials. Many of the districts attending these institutes had had no prior exposure to the curriculum materials being disseminated by the center (between 40% and 70%, depending on the grade level). At the center's initial institutes, district teams attended sessions designed to introduce them to the pedagogy of inquiry-based learning, heard presentations from publishers on specific curricula, and began planning a curriculum review process to be carried out when the team returned home. At the other end of the continuum, the SCI Center at BSCS chose to work intensively on adoption and implementation processes with districts already considering the adoption of reform-based materials.

All four centers engaged in spreading basic information about a high-quality science curriculum and engaging districts in the initial stages of planning curriculum reform (for instance, building leadership teams and planning the adoption process). Where center evaluations tracked these numbers, they reported that the dissemination centers reached or exceeded their original goals for the number and types of districts that would participate in basic dissemination activities.

The center evaluations looked at whether participants were aware of the kinds of inquiry-based materials advocated by the national science standards and promoted by the NSF and the centers. Most of the district team leaders involved with EDC's K–12 Center said they had heard that at least some of the curriculum materials had been disseminated by the center, though relatively few (38%) said that they had any firsthand experience with the materials. Districts were much more familiar and experienced with elementary curriculum materials than with materials developed for high schools.

Evaluations found that district teams and individual team members participated in dissemination center activities for a variety of reasons. EDC's K–12 Center review found that fewer than half of the participants (45%) attending center seminars reported that they had come as part of a planned improvement effort. Most participants (70% or more) attended for more general purposes—to gather information about a range of curriculum materials or keep abreast of developments in science education.

Two of the four dissemination center evaluations collected data from districts and estimated the number of districts participating in center activities that eventually adopted some of the science curriculum materials promoted by the centers. In both cases, center evaluators found that the number of districts that persisted through the stages of awareness, review, selection, adoption, and implementation was relatively small. About half of the districts that attended the centers' initial activities did not attend activities designed to support districts through later stages of the process. Of those that continued their work with the center, only some adopted materials within the lifetime of the project. For example, EDC's K–12 Center evaluation found that although 523 districts participated in awareness-raising and planning activities, only 243 went on to review materials on-site. Further into the process, 161 of the districts that EDC's K–12 Center worked with completed the full sequence of institutes and sessions to support implementation. Finally, 123 districts used the materials. The review of the SCI Center reported 19 districts participating in initial awareness-raising activities, while 10 districts completed all institutes or support sessions with 8 districts using materials. All four project evaluations reported that the number of districts completing the adoption and implementation of a new science curriculum was fewer than originally anticipated.

Insight Into Adoption of Curriculum Materials

Project evaluations offered some insight into why the numbers of districts ultimately adopting new curriculum materials were lower than originally anticipated. EDC's K–12 Center's evaluation found that larger districts, more affluent districts, and urban districts were more likely to end up reviewing, piloting, and adopting the exemplary curriculum materials. These patterns suggest that the availability of resources is a key factor in the adoption process: Larger districts and urban districts have larger budgets and better access to regional curriculum libraries and other resources that would support curriculum review, adoption, and implementation. More affluent districts typically face less stringent resource constraints. They are also less likely to be subject to the accountability pressures in literacy and mathematics that have diverted attention and other resources from science instruction in recent years.

Evaluations of all four dissemination centers suggest that curricular change is gradual. One evaluation concluded that the centers' work "is not as much about the adoption of a particular curriculum as it is about using the curriculum adoption process to foster incremental change in overall thinking about the science program and science instruction." Other evaluations noted that the centers' work was most effective in districts that had had some previous experience with science reform or some previous exposure to new curriculum materials. For example, districts involved with science reform efforts such as the NSF's Urban Systemic Initiatives often fared better than districts that had no such history. Similarly, districts already familiar with the materials disseminated by the centers before they attended a seminar were more likely to end up using new materials. One evaluation found that 27% of districts already familiar with EDC's K–12 Center's curriculum materials ended up piloting new materials, compared with 18% of districts that had had no previous exposure to new curriculum materials.

In some cases, creating this initial readiness for reform demanded all of the dissemination centers' available resources. Both the IMPACT and LASER Centers' evaluations reported that in states or regions where districts had relatively little experience with new curriculum materials, the centers concentrated heavily on strategic planning and awareness activities because districts were not yet ready to consider adoption. The LASER Center's regional partners, for example, worked primarily with districts that were new to science reform, with little attention paid to districts' needs for continued assistance as they worked to renew and sustain their programs.

Evaluations reported somewhat mixed news on district implementation of new materials. EDC's evaluation found that 65% of the districts that had purchased new curriculum materials had taken a series of steps considered by the center to be essential to implement them, such as establishing procedures for managing and storing materials or developing a strategy for classroom-based assessment. Among districts that used materials, about a third failed to provide some of the supports that the center deemed essential. Least likely to be provided were implementation supports that would cost money or would force trade-offs with other priorities, for example, providing ongoing professional development to teachers in both science content and pedagogy or setting aside adequate instructional time for science.

The Tales of Two School Districts in Colorado and Mississippi

The following are brief case studies of two very different school districts that worked with EDC's K–12 Science Curriculum Dissemination Center. Although different, the two had in common their commitment to a larger reform effort. In the case of Aguilar, Colorado, that effort was newly mandated state science standards; in Clinton, Mississippi, it was an assistant superintendent's vision for improving science education.

> *Aguilar, Colorado*
>
> - This is a very small, high-poverty, rural district, with no prior exposure to inquiry-based science.
> - Newly mandated state science standards prompted a review of the science curriculum, Grades K–9.
> - A core team of teachers and school administrators attended the full series of EDC's K–12 Center's seminars and worked closely with the regional hub's staff.
> - The district adopted the *Full Option Science System* (FOSS) in Grades K–6 in 2002–2003, with expansion to Grades 7–8 in 2003–2004.
>
> *Clinton, Mississippi*
>
> - This is a district of 5,000 students outside a larger metropolitan area.
> - The assistant superintendent committed to improving the quality of science instruction.
> - District teachers attended all six of EDC's K–12 Center's seminars offered in the region and two summer institutes.
> - With support from the regional hub, teacher buy-in was gained in the district.
> - The district adopted FOSS and *Science and Technology for Children* (STC) in Grades K–1 in 2002–2003 and *Insights in Biology* in Grade 9.
>
> Source: Policy Studies Associates, Inc. (2003, November). *Supporting the Adoption of Exemplary Science Curriculum Materials in Underserved Districts: Evaluation of the EDC K–12 Science Curriculum Dissemination Center.*

The evaluation of the SCI Center asked district team members to report on the extent to which the center had improved district capacity for curriculum reform. At the end of 3 years, 80% to 90% of team members reported that they had made substantial progress toward their original goals. Accomplishments most often cited by team members included the following:

- Improving teacher professional development
- Improving the process for choosing instructional materials
- Raising awareness of inquiry throughout the district
- Developing new leadership to help promote high school science reform

The SCI Center evaluation also reported, however, that teachers who piloted or implemented new curriculum materials reported mixed results, noting that they sometimes had trouble with the pacing of lessons and that students sometimes had trouble with the tasks required of them. One district reported difficulty aligning a curriculum across years. Although the centers had worked with district leadership teams to develop plans to address these challenges, teachers still struggled to make the materials "work" in their classrooms. The evaluation concluded that it would take more time to tell how successful most districts will be in their efforts to implement new instructional materials.

Promising Signs for Adoption and Implementation

Project evaluations (including the cross-center program evaluation) identified the following factors as important influences on districts' progress toward adoption and implementation of curriculum materials:

• District leadership. District-level case studies showed that district leadership, often the advocacy of a single person, was crucial to successful adoption and implementation of materials. In many districts, an assistant superintendent or a science curriculum coordinator facilitated the district's exploration of new science curricula. This person typically invested considerable time and resources in building support for adoption and implementation of the curricula. In Clinton, Mississippi, for example, the district's assistant superintendent for curriculum and instruction, observing the uneven quality of science instruction throughout the district, pulled together a team of teachers and a principal to rework the district's approach to teaching science. Over a period of 2 years, this science team, led by the assistant superintendent, reviewed the Mississippi science curriculum frameworks, solicited input from parents, selected new curriculum materials, piloted those materials, and worked to align their instruction with new state science assessments. The assistant superintendent collaborated with EDC's K–12 Center's regional hub to secure expert support and advice for the team, located funding to purchase new materials, and made sure that teachers were given time to work on challenges to implementation in the classroom in study team meetings.

• Teacher buy-in and beliefs about the value of the curriculum materials. Several evaluations noted that in school districts in which teachers believed that standards-based curriculum materials represented "good science," engaged the interest of their students, or offered a better alternative to their current instructional program, adoptions were more likely to be successful. Districts often used well-designed pilot programs as a strategy to expose teachers to the new materials and to secure their support for adoption.

- Previous experience with science reform. Several evaluations found that districts that had prior experience with a reform-oriented science curriculum were more likely to proceed through the process of reviewing, selecting, and implementing materials.

- Alignment of curriculum materials with state standards and assessments. Districts placed a high priority on selecting curriculum materials that were likely to improve student learning and students' performance on state assessments. As a result, the dissemination centers and regional hubs invested considerable time and energy in helping districts map the alignment of curriculum materials to state standards.

- Resources to support the purchase of materials, refurbishment of kits, and teacher professional development. One evaluation noted that districts had relied on funds from NSF programs such as the Urban Systemic Initiatives and Rural Systemic Initiatives as well as the former Eisenhower Professional Development Program to purchase new materials and to support teacher professional development related to implementation. Other evaluations noted that in districts in which local school boards and the superintendent supported the adoption of new science materials and funds were available, implementation proceeded relatively smoothly.

- Timing of the adoption cycle. When a district's participation in dissemination center activities coincided with a regularly scheduled textbook adoption, teams were much more likely to follow through with the kind of curriculum review envisioned by the centers. Several project evaluations noted that when the timing was off (for example, when district teams attended center activities the year after adopting new science materials), they were far less likely to act on the information the centers provided.

Barriers to Adoption and Implementation

Individual project evaluations and the cross-center evaluation also identified some barriers to implementation:

- *A lack of resources to support adoption and implementation of new materials.* These resources include funding for the purchase and maintenance of science kits at the elementary level and instructional time available for science.

- *Competing district priorities.* These priorities include the shift in recent years to a focus on literacy and math amid the testing and accountability requirements of the No Child Left Behind Act.
- *District turbulence.* Changing leadership or priorities can be a major barrier to curriculum reform.

Identifying Regional Capacity

As described above, three of the four centers worked to establish and strengthen a network of regional satellites to reach districts. Building the satellite centers was difficult, intensive work. In all three of the centers that operated regional satellites, several satellite centers were not able to fulfill their role as envisioned. The centers either found a new location or refocused their work on the remaining regional satellites that were functioning well.

Regional entities most successful in working with the centers were often housed in organizations whose own purposes were closely aligned with the mission of the science curriculum dissemination centers. University-based centers, regional education agencies, and organizations that had begun under earlier science education grants were often the most active and successful partners for the centers. This finding held true across the three centers that worked to develop a network of regional satellites. In this sense, the dissemination centers were engaged in identifying existing regional capacity and developing effective partnerships rather than building capacity where it did not exist before. The centers' experience with the regional satellites also demonstrates the cumulative effects of NSF investments: Many of the regional satellites had their roots in prior NSF programs.

For all of the centers, the demand for regional satellite services far outstripped available resources. Case studies of individual districts conducted for project evaluations featured intensive support and consultation by regional staff. However, all of the evaluations found that regional satellites were able to provide this level of support in only a few instances. More often, follow-up services were much more limited.

The centers worked to build regional capacity in a variety of ways. They helped regional satellites establish curriculum libraries and oriented staff to the new materials. EDC's K–12 Center, for example, held several satellite leader meetings to familiarize regional staff with the contents and design of the curriculum materials disseminated by the center. Several evaluations noted that housing curriculum libraries where local educators could actually see the materials at the heart of the program was one of the most important functions of the regional satellites. In addition, regional centers said that hosting the curriculum libraries was an important benefit of their partnership with the centers. At the SCI Center at BSCS, staff members worked on building local leadership capacity and developed implementation models that examined the ingredients involved in getting reform-based materials implemented across an entire school system.

At the IMPACT Center, working with regional satellites involved developing a cadre of 300 curriculum trainers (typically, classroom teachers with experience and special training in the use of standards-based curriculum materials) to provide professional development to teachers in schools and districts implementing new curriculum materials. The IMPACT Center developed a course of training and a certification process for curriculum trainers in the region and also collaborated with regional sites to provide that training to teachers. The project evaluation identified the curriculum trainers as an important regional resource but noted that because so many of them were current classroom teachers, their availability for training was typically limited to the summer or just a few days during the school year. The IMPACT Center also provided funding to regional satellites for one or more implementation advisors, who provided individual consultation and other support for curriculum adoption to districts in their regions as needed. The project evaluation, however, found that the role of the implementation advisor was not well defined or consistent across satellites. The evaluation reported that satellite staff serving as advisors expressed frustration with their role and struggled to identify ways they could support districts effectively.

A unique feature of the LASER Center's strategy for building regional capacity was its emphasis on creating regional partnerships—formal organizations of regional leaders from businesses, universities, museums, foundations, and state agencies. These regional partnerships developed a broad base of support for science reform in their regions and leveraged additional funding to implement and sustain effective science programs. In Washington State, for example, a partnership of leading science institutions and key businesses advocated for science reform and helped to deliver training and other support to districts. The LASER Center conducted a planning retreat in each of eight regions to help establish the partnerships. However, because the demand for strategic planning institutes—the initial planning and awareness-raising institutes offered by the LASER Center itself—was higher than expected, LASER focused less on developing and supporting regional partnerships than originally planned. The project evaluation reported that at the end of the grant period, regional partnerships were operating successfully in four of the eight LASER Center regions.

When satellite center staff described the benefits of affiliating with the centers, they often pointed to the benefits of having access to sample curriculum materials and expertise in helping districts to review, adopt, and plan for curriculum implementation, and they reported that their affiliation with the dissemination centers had given science educators in their regions access to high-quality, standards-based curriculum materials for the first time. In addition, affiliation with the dissemination centers helped burnish their reputation in the region as a valuable source of information and assistance for cutting-edge reform in science education. As one of EDC's K–12 Center hub leader reported: "It's useful for us to be connected to EDC, especially with our reports to the [state] Board of Regents. It really helps. It gives a national perspective as one of [the] hubs. We're playing in a league that [the state] doesn't play in. . . . We've learned a lot from EDC."

Project evaluations found that beyond the end of the NSF grant period, the future of the regional satellites as self-sustaining entities was uncertain. Some regional center leaders noted that future funding for the regional center was not secure and that a fee structure that would make the regional satellites self-sufficient was not possible for most of the districts in their region. In some cases, then, the region intermediaries cultivated by the dissemination centers appeared unlikely to carry the efforts forward beyond the life of the project.

Summary and Conclusion

Evaluations found that the science dissemination centers worked at three levels: (1) a broad awareness level in which the centers helped many districts gain an introductory knowledge of NSF curricula; (2) an intermediate level in which the centers offered extended materials showcases, workshops, and other support to help districts engage in a deliberate process of curriculum selection; and, in more limited cases, (3) an in-depth level where the centers worked with districts to support the process of curriculum selection and implementation over a longer period of time.

All four center evaluations found that although the science dissemination centers had succeeded in developing some high-quality awareness-raising activities as well as training for curriculum selection that was much valued by participating districts, their success in helping districts follow through with solid implementation of new materials was more mixed. The cross-center program evaluation found that NSF-funded dissemination and implementation centers had contributed to the use of standards-based materials by (a) exposing more districts and schools to standards-based science curriculum materials and to inquiry-based instructional approaches; (b) providing districts with greater access to standards-based materials, particularly for many districts that had no other means; (c) encouraging a more systematic and thoughtful selection process for materials; and (d) building up networks of staff developers and others to assist districts and schools in the selection and adoption process.

In the course of their work, all four dissemination and implementation centers encountered huge variations in the capacity of districts to engage in science reform, in teachers' knowledge of and faith in the new curriculum materials, in the supports and constraints of their local contexts, and in their readiness to pursue a curriculum-centered improvement strategy. As a result, project evaluations concluded that the work of the centers was more about building the capacity to select and implement a standards-based curriculum than the implementation itself.

All educational innovations must take into account district and school readiness and prior experience with reform, as well as the time needed for teachers to learn about new materials and approaches to instruction. In addition, standards-based science curriculum materials such as those disseminated by the centers require high levels of teacher content knowledge, ongoing teacher professional development, and systems for managing and replenishing classroom kits and modules that were often more resource intensive than traditional textbook-based curricula. The dissemination and implementation centers attempted to help district leadership teams increase their knowledge of science and of science teaching and reform, so that gradually the district context would become more supportive of an inquiry-based, student-centered instructional approach.

For their part, the cases of Aguilar, Colorado, and Clinton, Mississippi, illustrate that any type of district can have success—the school system need not be large or flush with resources. In addition, both districts benefited from the external support (training, materials, personal relationships) provided by EDC's K–12 Center and its regional hubs. That arrangement eventually bore fruit, but the adoption process took time. According to the evaluation of the center, both the Aguilar and Clinton districts benefited from repeated exposure to the new curriculum materials and ideas about teaching science.

One evaluation team concluded its report this way: "The process of curricular change is slow and incremental. It is a multi-step process.... Thus, we conclude that the [dissemination center's work] is not as much about the adoption of a particular curriculum as it is about using the curriculum adoption process to foster incremental change in overall thinking about the science program and science instruction."

7

Using the Centers' Work to Improve Science Education

Some Practical Advice

Millicent Lawton, Barbara Brauner Berns, and Judith Opert Sandler

Education Development Center, Inc.

In the decade after the national science standards were first published in 1996, reforms aimed at improving teaching and learning took many tacks. Some nationally recognized and well-regarded efforts envisioned professional development as the crux of change across subject areas. Other models used specific instructional strategies or assessment as a focus. By contrast, this book describes a major effort to improve science education that saw curriculum—specifically, a particular type of exemplary instructional materials—as the linchpin of reform.

The exemplary materials became the focal point for a process designed to (a) lead educators to define the goals of local science programs, (b) see the materials selection process as an opportunity to grow professionally, (c) rethink other areas of classroom practice such as assessment, and (d) build professional development that complemented the content and teaching strategies in the chosen curriculum. The centers learned that such an approach asks schools and educators to do some of the hardest work possible: to undertake an intensive upgrade of their science education programs using cutting-edge methods and materials. Embracing the standards-based materials took participants out of their comfort zones—what they were used to hearing, saying, and doing—and asked them to make changes using tools they may not have seen before and about which they often had many questions. Adding to the centers' challenge was an education infrastructure usually ill-equipped to support ongoing curriculum improvement efforts with funding or expertise.

Taken together, the centers' experience shows that an effort to upgrade curriculum is a monumental undertaking that can't work with the usual approaches or the traditional resources that are devoted to getting curriculum materials into the nation's public school classrooms. In committing to curriculum reform, it is best to acknowledge such challenges at the outset. For instance, addressing worries or skeptical questions from educators and others can result in a rich, provocative, and productive discussion. Based on the centers' work, issues that could arise range from the value of the inquiry-based approach of the instructional materials to possible mismatches with existing state tests.

Despite the problems they encountered, the centers' achievements live on today, showing that lasting changes are possible. For example, as mentioned in Chapter 3, the Boston public schools have clearly benefited from work done by both the IMPACT Center and the SCI Center. Today, all curriculum-based professional development in the district is designed and delivered by teacher leaders trained by center consultants. Meanwhile, an outgrowth of EDC's K–12 Center's work, the Northern Indiana Science, Math, and Engineering Collaborative, was created through a federal Math-Science Partnership grant awarded by the state education department. The collaborative is working regionally to provide intensive professional development—35 hours a year for 3 years—focused on implementing an inquiry-based curriculum. As mentioned in Chapter 4, the legacy of the centers' work on assessment lives on in locations as disparate as Delaware, South Dakota, and Washington State. And from the city of San Diego to rural communities in Mississippi, the time spent working through curriculum, assessment, and professional development issues produced stronger science education, deeper administrative support for innovative teaching, and a lasting view of curriculum as a powerful driver of school improvement work.

Getting Down to Business: Seeking Support

If the work of the centers showed anything, it is that local school districts cannot achieve a comprehensive upgrade in science teaching and learning without some help. External support can help ease the initial selection and subsequent implementation of the curriculum materials, as well as make them more educationally sound. It can also help sustain the reform: The creation of infrastructure—systems and practices—and the building of capacity can make it possible for reforms to endure. An outside catalyst for change can add credibility to an effort that can be undermined by criticism that it is the work of a small group of internal crusaders.

Depending on the size of the system taking on curriculum-led reforms, seeking support can mean many things: (a) hiring external consultants, (b) reaching out to state agencies, (c) taking part in a consortium supported by outside funding, (d) affiliating with a research university or regional technical assistance entity, (e) partnering with schools or school districts that have experience with these kinds of changes, or (f) some combination of these. When larger partnerships are not practical, one alternative is to find or create a leadership cadre or resource group locally. That group could obtain the training needed to assume further capacity building in a district or group of districts. The important thing is to have help, not who does the helping; if homegrown assistance is available, so much the better.

The centers' work demonstrated that districts and their outside partners should have two main categories of work in mind: *substance* and *support*. Substance means ensuring that the curriculum materials, assessments, and professional development are standards and research based, that they are a learning experience in themselves, and that they are aligned, to the extent possible, with state standards and requirements. The preceding chapters address those issues extensively.

Meanwhile, support covers everything else. That includes, for example, involving key people, obtaining buy-in, allocating adequate fiscal and other resources for the changes to succeed, and countering skepticism and stasis. It also means creating communities of practice, giving advice on how to manage and maintain science kits, scheduling adequate time for learning, and establishing policies that spell out expectations and provisions for follow-through. The centers found that these are among the critical factors that can spell triumph or doom for the successful selection and implementation of curriculum materials that could lead to improved student achievement.

Despite its need for support, the school district's role is absolutely pivotal. Just as the role of those providing assistance is to *build* capacity to help schools implement and sustain curriculum-driven change, it is the role of the school districts to step up and *supply* capacity, in whatever quantity and quality possible. Sometimes, individuals within a district or a school already have the needed expertise. A district's relationship with an assisting agency must be a partnership; there are responsibilities and tasks for the outside partner, and there are responsibilities and tasks for the district. Individual schools and principals must also take an active role, with any school-based decision making and local accountability structures factored in.

Addressing Substance: Action Steps

Based on the work of the four science curriculum centers, certain issues emerge for organizations that are considering trying to do similar work. The lessons learned by the centers in all kinds of school settings can be distilled into the aforementioned broad categories of substance and support. In tackling the substance of curriculum-led reforms, the lessons learned by the centers apply not only to the school systems but also to the assisting agencies or resource groups working with them.

Make Selection and Implementation of a Curriculum an Analytical and Educative Experience

Curriculum selection should be an inquiry process, fostering opportunities for adult learning, with teachers involved throughout the entire process. Because educators make the key decisions about choosing a curriculum, they should discuss content and performance standards, analyze assessments and achievement data, and examine both their own teaching methods and those of others. This can occur through activities such as summer seminars, hands-on learning experiences (pulled from the materials themselves), lesson study, or all of the above.

Monitor Fidelity of Implementation of the Instructional Materials

The curriculum materials described in this book have been carefully designed and field-tested and should be used as intended; teachers are not advised to pick and choose among features or activities and jettison the rest (to do so imperils students' thorough development of concepts). In addition, teachers often start out using materials in a mechanical way or trying to mix the "old way" with the "new way," such as by intermingling desirable hands-on activities with less ideal vocabulary drills. They may need to be helped to move toward a deeper level of use or a fuller understanding of why, for instance, the materials call for fewer topics to be taught in greater depth than most textbooks do.

Carefully Define—and Redefine, if Necessary—What Professional Development Means

School district personnel may not be familiar with the components of high-quality professional development (PD) because the quality of PD can vary considerably across the country. In the most successful model developed around the standards- and research-based curricula described in this book, professional development—at its best—occurred over months, not days; was built into teachers' regular jobs and work hours; and related directly to their daily work, particularly to the content knowledge and pedagogy necessary to successfully implement instructional materials.

Provide Multiple Opportunities for Participants to Develop Expertise

Good teachers know that some students need to hear—or experience—something more than once before they "get it." It should not be a surprise, then, that that is also true for adults learning to use innovative instructional materials. Build in repeated exposures to the materials and the methods for using them, as well as opportunities to ask follow-up questions and try things again in a new way.

Expect Assessment to Be a Challenge

Exemplary curriculum materials require teachers to use what may be unfamiliar methods of collecting and interpreting evidence about what students know and can do. Consider having teachers who are familiar with the new materials model both teaching and assessment strategies. Also, make use of the tools and resources that exist to aid with classroom assessment, understanding that exemplary materials employ best practices—and challenging new ideas—in many areas of classroom learning.

Coordinate Work on Science Curriculum With Other Parts of the Education System

Align science curriculum materials with state standards and assessments, but also make connections with other disciplines and departments, from math and reading to libraries or media centers and offices of special needs or English-language learning. Look into how federal or state grant money can be used for science, and assign science educators or local scientists to advisory boards or management councils to assist with implementation of new materials. If other reforms are occurring locally, integrate changes in science with those efforts, making sure the goals, indicators of success, and philosophies of learning and pedagogy are as compatible as possible.

Addressing Support: Action Steps

When it comes to issues of support, the steps indicated by the centers' work differ for school systems and outside partners or local resource groups. Steps for each group, respectively, follow.

Local school districts need to do the following:

- *Devote resources to this work, including money and time.* There must be a willingness and a commitment to provide ample resources; otherwise, the work is likely to stall. Funds must be set aside not only to purchase instructional materials and refresh science kits but also to pay for teacher professional development. Time is equally important. In the short term, teachers need release time to take part in selection committee meetings or PD seminars, for example. In the longer view, comprehensive changes need to be given time—measured in years, not months or weeks—to take hold. When there is no way to add time or money, there must be a commitment to reallocating existing resources.

- *Provide committed leadership.* The centers' experiences showed that changes in district administration or school leadership are likely during the course of a multiyear project. If the key leaders who change positions are the main forces behind the project, it can quickly falter. The centers found that it is essential to have local leaders who believe in the work and can shepherd it over a period of years. Sometimes, those people are administrators, teachers, or a combination of the two. Often, the strong advocacy of a single person can make a major difference. However, a team of leaders who can survive the departure of the chief advocate ensures a better chance of stability and continuity over the time frame required for major change.

- *Foster a willingness to accept innovation and assistance.* One of the biggest hurdles to overcome in using the innovative materials and methods at the heart of the centers' work is changing entrenched ways and mind-sets. The centers found that a school district with previous experience in science reform was more likely to be open to exemplary instructional materials. However, even without prior exposure, committed leaders can pave the way for receptivity and success.

> **Notable Quote**
>
> "To establish such deep philosophical change with teachers who've been in their school districts doing their thing that they think they're doing well requires working in a focused way on many fronts," said Karen Morris of the University of Notre Dame, who was a leader of EDC's K–12 Center's northern Indiana hub. "My enthusiasm for the project kept me from seeing the difficulty that was there. Looking back, I see the need to understand the differences in personalities and contexts that make each district different and create a need to, even, see each school in an individualistic way. You also have to work with educators so they don't see change as something they take personally but see it as a way to think and interact professionally. As we work, though, we keep finding supporters even in unusual places, like counselors, nurses, or art teachers. This kind of work constantly offers challenges but also plenty of ways to feel encouraged by what you can see happening."

For their part, outside partners or resource groups (whether at the local, state, regional, or national level) need to do the following:

- *Act as a bridge between those with expertise in the instructional materials and the schools and educators who need to use them.* The better the communication about the intent behind the goals of a reform effort or a given set of instructional materials, the more likely they will be implemented as envisioned. By working to make sure new materials are adopted and used, the outside partner also gains insight into the reality the educators face—good and bad—when trying to use the materials.

- *Be aware of and acknowledge local capabilities and attitudes.* Be realistic, and don't work based on what you assume to be true. Educators and others involved in new initiatives will come from different backgrounds and have varying levels of education, motivation, and interest, which can make training a challenge. Some may be starting from a very basic level of understanding or familiarity. Initially, the assistance provided may need to focus on basic use of the materials, not on mastery. Changing minds and familiar ways is not easy. However, the centers found that when treated as hard and serious work, it can, and does, happen.

- *Foster familiarity and comfort with materials.* In the experience of the centers, these are the keys to winning over educators. Giving demonstrations and holding showcases where teachers, principals, and others can see students and teachers using the instructional materials and even use the materials themselves in adult learning sessions can be a promising start. In addition, professional developers may want to reinforce messages about the curricula by making classroom visits, showing videos featuring teachers using the materials, and encouraging teachers to attend state and national meetings hosted by such professional organizations as the National Science Teachers Association.

- *Consider bringing groups of schools or districts together.* In small or rural districts, creating a network of districts can help ease problems with leadership capacity or resource allocation. Within a very large urban district, by contrast, creating a smaller alliance of schools inside the big system can facilitate communication, team building, and learning.

- *Beware of competing priorities, changing priorities, or changing leadership.* One example of competing priorities is that created by the No Child Left Behind (NCLB) law and the mandate placed first on testing in reading and mathematics. The NCLB requirement to test all students in Grades 3–8 annually in reading and math—with improvement goals for many subgroups of a school's student body—forced many states to focus on those subjects. Both anecdotal and factual evidence since then have indicated that time and resources devoted to other subject areas, such as science, were squeezed to a minimum—or eliminated entirely—as a result. This nationwide reality compounded the challenge the centers faced in encouraging schools and districts to tackle an intensive, nontraditional upgrade of science education programs.

    o Now that federally mandated testing has turned to science, those tests may exert a different, strong influence on science

curricula and instruction. For good or ill, the influence will almost certainly be a disproportionate one; the examinations required by NCLB will account for a small fraction of the total time spent on science and science assessments. Meanwhile, a growing trend among states to give statewide end-of-course exams as part of measures of student competency may also increasingly shape science programs.
- Other school reform efforts may also bring new challenges and opportunities for science education. For example, a recent push nationally to add "rigor" and "relevance" to high schools—in part, encouraging students to take more challenging courses—may put pressure on schools and districts to rethink teaching and learning and requirements for the number and type of science courses students should take.

- *Help develop a wider infrastructure for improvement of science education.* The improvement efforts needed are too sweeping to be limited to those housed in local school districts. Some school districts have made, or will make, a relatively big investment in improvement—in the same way that individual teaching hospitals invest in improving young doctors' practice of medicine. But those cannot be the only locations for the creation of improvement infrastructure. Instead, coordinated efforts should exist at the national, regional, state, and local levels. Indeed, in issuing draft recommendation for improving science, technology, engineering, and mathematics (STEM) education, a commission of the National Science Board recently called for a "national coordinating body" to oversee federal spending in this area and to match up that work with state and regional efforts. The draft report also recommended requiring states to create "P-20 councils" that would manage STEM education efforts from prekindergarten through the graduate level.

Connecting With Research

One aspect of building a national improvement infrastructure for pre-collegiate science education is to support research into related topics. Many issues in science teaching and learning bear investigating. Here are just a few needed research questions:

- Are there ways to increase the inadequate supply of science teachers?
- How can science teachers be effectively prepared, supported, inducted, and retained?

- What enables teachers to deliver the kind of inquiry-based, active science education envisioned by the national science standards?
- Are cutting-edge, standards-based instructional materials in science implemented with fidelity to their original design?
- How has the No Child Left Behind Act affected assessment of students in science and, in turn, classroom teaching?
- What is the effect of standards-based science materials on teachers' levels of engagement, and what, in turn, does that do to student achievement?
- For which students does achievement improve and why?
- How can instructional materials, as a statement of a school's expectations for science content and learning experiences, connect to professional development?
- Does using exemplary materials influence teacher turnover?

Being Aware of the Context

Despite the best efforts of local school districts and their outside partners, there will always be contextual factors beyond their control. Some of these issues that came to light in the centers' work are discussed below.

The Timing of the Adoption Cycle

Roughly half of all states conduct statewide adoptions of instructional materials. If the introduction of the exemplary instructional materials coincides with or precedes a new adoption cycle, the materials are much more likely to be seriously considered and/or implemented than if science educators are exposed to new materials just *after* an adoption.

The Need to Improve Preservice Teacher Preparation and Revise State Requirements for Licensure

To address issues of teacher quality and educational equity, better alignment is needed between what is required of science teachers when they enter the classroom and their preservice preparation. The inconsistent quality of teacher preparation programs nationwide and the wide variation among state requirements for certification mean that student learning experiences vary widely (and inequitably) and professional developers must scramble to address gaps in teachers'

The Existence of Mandated Large-Scale Student Achievement Testing and School Accountability Policies

As mentioned in Chapter 4, the national stampede toward high-stakes, large-scale assessments threatens to trample the use of standards-based instructional materials that support such alternative classroom assessments as journal entries, discussions, or drawings. State and national testing also tend to narrow how educators interpret the message of "standards." Yet the centers did manage to align local use of the cutting-edge instructional materials with state standards and assessment systems.

Summary and Conclusion

The lessons and action steps outlined above could not have come about without the 5 (or more) years of work of each of the four science curriculum dissemination and implementation centers funded by the NSF, beginning in the late 1990s. Using the organizing themes of substance and support, this chapter has attempted to give practical guidance to those interested in initiating or continuing similar work focused on encouraging the adoption and use of standards- and research-based curriculum materials.

In the wake of the release of national standards in science education, the question was, Could the NSF, through the centers, make progress toward ensuring that school districts selected and used exemplary science instructional materials, K–12? Clearly, they did make progress, some of which is still in effect today. But the intent behind such work went beyond the relatively narrow challenge of getting the curricula into the districts. The exemplary instructional materials were also an entry point for trying to make changes on two broader fronts: advancing systemic reform (such as transforming teacher professional development and assessment) and improving the science achievement and science literacy of students through inquiry-based methods.

In those areas, as well as in the selection and use of exemplary materials, much work remains to be done. Textbooks still dominate in U.S. science classrooms, and the curriculum is still a "mile wide and an inch deep," as the Third International Mathematics and Science Study's researchers famously said a decade ago. PreK–16 science education (or, arguably, preK–20) is still not viewed as a curricular continuum in the way that it must be to ensure that it is comprehensive, is cohesive, and provides scaffolding of ideas while avoiding repetition and superficiality.

However daunting the task may seem, it is doable. The effort begins with commitment—a few individuals pledging themselves and the resources to making a change.

Anyone trying to engage in this type of reform needs to be clear on one more thing: Whatever plan is made, it's going to change. This work must be done with an attitude of flexibility, not rigidity. Reformers must understand that frustrations and failure are part of the process and realize that failure is one of the chief ways that learning—and, eventually, success—occurs.

It remains to be seen whether the United States is on the verge of a full-fledged campaign to improve science education. But given the global marketplace for jobs and the lightning speed of advances in science and technology, the need for profound and prolonged attention to increasing the science literacy and proficiency of American students becomes more critical with each passing day. We don't need just more scientists and engineers; we need people who appreciate and understand science well enough to be fully engaged citizens.

Appendix I

Standards-Based Curriculum Materials Disseminated by EDC's K–12 Science Center

This list of materials is meant to be representative but not exhaustive. All materials were available as of October 2007.

Active Physics
Publisher: It's About Time
Developer: Arthur Eisenkraft
Date of publication: 1999
Grade levels: 9–12
Scientific domain: Physics
Web site: www.its-about-time.com/htmls/ap.html

ARIES: Astronomy-Based Physical Science
Publisher: Charlesbridge Publishing
Developer: Harvard-Smithsonian Center for Astrophysics
Date of publication: 2000
Grade levels: 3–8
Scientific domains: Physical science, earth and space science
Web site: www.charlesbridge.com/school/html/aries.html

Biology: A Community Context
Publisher: Glencoe/McGraw-Hill
Developers: William Leonard and John Penick
Date of publication: 2003
Grade levels: 9–10

Scientific domain: Biology
Web site: www.glencoe.com/sec/science/biology/bacc/index.html

BSCS Biology: A Human Approach
Publisher: Kendall/Hunt Publishing
Developer: BSCS
Date of publication: 2006 (3rd edition)
Grade levels: 9–12
Scientific domain: Biology
Web sites: www.kendallhunt.com/index.cfm?PID=219&PGI=143 and www.bscs.org/curriculumdevelopment/highschool/comprehensive/human

BSCS Biology: A Molecular Approach (Blue Version)
Publisher: Glencoe/McGraw-Hill
Developer: BSCS
Date of publication: 2006 (9th edition)
Grade levels: High school
Scientific domain: Biology
Web sites: www.glencoe.com/catalog/index.php/program?c=1674&s=8454&p=4162 and www.bscs.org/curriculumdevelopment/highschool/comprehensive/molecular

BSCS Biology: An Ecological Approach (Green Version)
Publisher: Kendall/Hunt Publishing
Developer: BSCS
Date of publication: 2006, 10th edition
Grade levels: High school
Scientific domain: Biology
Web sites: www.kendallhunt.com/index.cfm?PID=219&PGI=144 and www.bscs.org/curriculumdevelopment/highschool/comprehensive/ecological

BSCS Science and Technology
Publisher: Kendall/Hunt Publishing
Developer: BSCS
Date of publication: 2005 (3rd edition)
Grade levels: 6–9
Scientific domains: Earth science, life science, physical science
Web sites: www.kendallhunt.com/index.cfm?PID=219&PGI=200 and www.bscs.org/curriculumdevelopment/middle/comprehensive/scitech

BSCS Science Tracks: Connecting Science and Literacy
Publisher: Kendall/Hunt Publishing
Developer: BSCS
Date of publication: 2006 (2nd edition)
Grade levels: K–5
Scientific domains: Physical science, life science, earth and space science, science and technology
Web sites: www.kendallhunt.com/tracks and www.bscs.org/curriculumdevelopment/elementary/tracks

Chemistry in the Community (ChemCom)
Publisher: W. H. Freeman
Developer: American Chemical Society
Date of publication: 2006 (5th edition)
Grade levels: 9–12
Scientific domain: Chemistry
Web sites: www.whfreeman.com/chemcom and www.acs.org

Developmental Approaches in Science, Health, and Technology (DASH)
Publisher: Curriculum Research and Development Group, University of Hawaii
Developer: Curriculum Research and Development Group, University of Hawaii
Date of publication: 2000
Grade levels: K–6
Scientific domains: Physical science, earth science, space science
Web site: www.hawaii.edu/crdg/programs/science.html

Earth System Science in the Community (EarthComm)
Publisher: It's About Time
Developer: Michael Smith, American Geological Institute
Date of publication: 1999–2002
Grade levels: 9–12
Scientific domain: Earth science
Web sites: www.its-about-time.com/htmls/ec.html and www.agiweb.org/earthcomm/about.html

Event-Based Science (EBS)
Publisher: Pearson Prentice Hall
Developer: Russell Wright, Montgomery County (MD) Public Schools
Date of publication: 1995–2004

Grade levels: 6–9
Scientific domains: Earth science, life science, physical science
Web sites: www.phschool.com/EBS and www.ebsinstitute.com

Foundational Approaches to Science Teaching (FAST)
Publisher: Curriculum Research and Development Group, University of Hawaii
Developer: Curriculum Research and Development Group, University of Hawaii
Date of publication: 1996 (latest edition)
Grade levels: 7–9
Scientific domains: Physics, chemistry, earth science, and biology content is organized into three strands: physical science, ecology, and relational study
Web site: www.hawaii.edu/crdg/programs/science.html

Foundations of Physical Science
Publisher: CPO Science
Developer: CPO Science
Date of publication: 2002
Grade levels: 9–12
Scientific domain: Physical science
Web site: www.cpo.com/tp_fps_entry.shtml

Full Option Science Systems (FOSS)
Publisher: Delta Education, Inc.
Developer: Lawrence Hall of Science, University of California at Berkeley
Date of publication: 2000
Grade levels: K–6
Scientific domains: Earth science, life science, physical science
Web sites: www.delta-education.com/science/foss/index.shtml and www.lawrencehallofscience.org/foss

Full Option Science Systems (FOSS) for Middle Schools
Publisher: Delta Education, Inc.
Developer: Lawrence Hall of Science, University of California at Berkeley
Date of publication: 2000–2003
Grade levels: 6–8
Scientific domains: Life science, earth science, physical science, technology

Web sites: www.delta-education.com/science/foss/mscomponents.shtml and www.lawrencehallofscience.org/foss

Insights
Publisher: Kendall/Hunt Publishing
Developer: Education Development Center, Inc.
Date of publication: 2003–2006 (2nd edition)
Grade levels: K–6
Scientific domains: Earth science, life science, physical science
Web sites: www.kendallhunt.com/insights and cse.edc.org/curriculum/insightsElem

Insights in Biology
Publisher: Kendall/Hunt Publishing
Developer: Education Development Center, Inc.
Date of publication: 2007 (2nd edition)
Grade levels: 9–10
Scientific domain: Biology
Web sites: www.kendallhunt.com/insightsinbiology and cse.edc.org/curriculum/insightsBiology

Investigating Earth Systems (IES)
Publisher: It's About Time
Developer: American Geological Institute
Date of publication: Fall 2000
Grade levels: 6–8
Scientific domain: Earth science
Web sites: www.its-about-time.com/htmls/ies.html and www.agiweb.org/ies/

Investigations in Environmental Science
Publisher: It's About Time
Developer: Northwestern University
Date of publication: 2005
Grade levels: 9–12
Scientific domain: Environmental science
Web sites: www.its-about-time.com/htmls/investines/inves.html and www.geode.northwestern.edu/investigations

Issues and Earth Science (IAES)
[See Science Education for Public Understanding Program (SEPUP)]

Issues, Evidence, and You (IEY)
[See Science Education for Public Understanding Program (SEPUP)]

Minds on Physics
Publisher: Kendall/Hunt Publishing
Developer: UMASS Physics Education Research Group
Date of publication: 1999–2003
Grade levels: 11–12
Scientific domain: Physics
Web sites: umperg.physics.umass.edu/resources/mop and www.kendall hunt.com/mindsonphysics

Science and Life Issues (SALI)
[See Science Education for Public Understanding (SEPUP)]

Science and Sustainability (S&S)
[See Science Education for Public Understanding (SEPUP)]

Science and Technology for Children (STC)
Publisher: Carolina Biological Supply Company
Developer: National Science Resources Center (NSRC)
Date of publication: 1997
Grade levels: 1–6
Scientific domains: Earth science, life science, physical science, technology
Web sites: www.nsrconline.org/curriculum_resources/elementary.html and www.carolinacurriculum.com/stc/index.asp

Science and Technology Concepts for Middle Schools (STC/MS)
Publisher: Carolina Biological Supply Company
Developer: National Science Resources Center
Dates of publication: 2000, 2003
Grade levels: 6–8
Scientific domains: Life science, earth science, physical science, technology
Web sites: www.nsrconline.org/curriculum_resources/middle_school .html and www.carolinacurriculum.com/stcms/index.asp

Science Education for Public Understanding Program (SEPUP)
[Includes Issues and Earth Science (IAES); Issues, Evidence, and You (IEY); Science and Life Issues (SALI); and Science and Sustainability (S&S)]
Publisher: Lab-Aids, Inc.

Developer: Lawrence Hall of Science, University of California at Berkeley
Dates of publication: 1992, 1996–1998, 2001–2003
Grade levels: 6–12
Scientific domains: Earth science, life science, physical science
Web site: www.sepup.com

Science in a Technical World
Publisher: W. H. Freeman
Developer: American Chemical Society
Date of publication: 2000
Grade levels: 9–12
Scientific domain: Integrated
Web sites: www.whfreeman.com/stw and www.acs.org/education

Appendix II

EDC's K–12 Science Center's Curriculum Selection and Curriculum Evaluation Process

To guide a district's or school's curriculum selection process, EDC's K–12 Science Center outlined three critical tasks, each with four steps. This process assumes that a district or school has clarified its goals for student learning through a set of standards or frameworks specifying expectations for student learning, including both conceptual knowledge and important skills.

Task 1: Identify criteria for looking at materials.

Step 1. Identify and assemble a team for reviewing materials.

Step 2. Examine existing evaluation tools and criteria.

Step 3. Select criteria based on program goals and local course of study.

Step 4. Create customized evaluation tool with agreed-upon criteria.

Task 2: Analyze materials for alignment with framework or course of study.

Step 1. Determine the concepts, topics, and skills emphasized in the new materials at each grade level.

Step 2. Compare materials to local standards and frameworks.

Step 3. Highlight strengths and weaknesses of materials based on criteria of customized evaluation tool.

Step 4. Justify or reject the materials based on their alignment.

Task 3: Get some firsthand experience with the materials.

Step 1. Gather new materials being considered.

Step 2. Identify internal and external teachers with experience using the materials.

Step 3. Convene leadership group to try out materials.

Step 4. Plan professional development opportunity to try out materials.

The curriculum evaluation tool, below, completes the EDC process for selecting instructional materials. This tool asks pertinent questions about the instructional materials and expects those examining the materials to support their answers to the questions with evidence. Categories of review include science content, instructional design, organization of teacher's materials, assessment, equity, and alignment with standards.

Curriculum Evaluation Tool

Name of Curriculum _____

Category/Question	*Evidence*
Content	
1. How appropriate is the content for the designated age level? Provide evidence.	
2. How significant and relevant to students' daily lives is the content? Provide evidence.	
3. Other	
Instructional Design	
4. Is scientific investigation taught, modeled, and practiced where appropriate? Provide evidence.	
5. Do the materials actively engage the students to promote their understanding of the content? Provide evidence.	
6. Are there sufficient experiences and opportunities for discussion for students to develop a deep understanding of content? Provide evidence.	
7. Other	

Category/Question	Evidence
Organization of Teacher's Materials	
8. Do the teacher's materials include clear and adequate background information? Provide evidence.	
9. Are there clear and adequate guidelines to support teaching all aspects of the lessons? Provide evidence.	
10. Are the format and structure of the teacher's materials easy for a teacher to follow?	
11. What special facilities and equipment are needed to implement the program?	
12. Other	
Assessment	
13. Are assessments for both students and teachers included in the materials? Provide evidence.	
14. Are there a variety of formal and informal assessments? Provide evidence.	
15. Other	
Equity	
16. Is the material free of racial, ethnic, gender, and age bias?	
17. Are appropriate strategies included to meet the needs of special/diverse populations? Provide evidence.	
18. Other	
Alignment With Standards	
19. How does the content align with district and state standards and frameworks for scientific knowledge? Provide evidence.	
20. How does the content align with district and state standards and frameworks for science thinking skills? Provide evidence.	
21. Other	

Source: © Education Development Center, Inc., 2003.

Appendix III

IMPACT Curriculum Review Panel MST
Instructional Materials Evaluation Tool

IMPACT Curriculum Review Panel
MST Instructional Materials Evaluation Tool

Name: _____ Publisher: _____ Pub. Yr.: _____ Grade: _____

1. STUDENT EXPERIENCES

To what extent do students' experiences . . .	Not at all	Inadequately	Adequately	Strongly	Exceptionally
1. involve them in inquiry-based learning and problem solving? (emphasize "doing" science or mathematics)					
Cite evidence from the materials to support your rating.					
2. enable them to investigate important scientific or mathematical concepts?					
Cite evidence from the materials to support your rating.					
3. provide multiple pathways to develop concepts and communicate ideas and solutions?					
Cite evidence from the materials to support your rating.					
4. include the use of manipulatives and tools to explore, model, and analyze situations and communicate findings? (noncomputer or computer-based)					
Cite evidence from the materials to support your rating.					

To what extent do students' experiences . . .	Not at all	Inadequately	Adequately	Strongly	Exceptionally
5. foster collaboration within the classroom?					
Cite evidence from the materials to support your rating.					
6. foster reflection on experiences and observations?					
Cite evidence from the materials to support your rating.					
7. attend to diverse cultural and economic backgrounds?					
Cite evidence from the materials to support your rating.					
8. provide developmentally appropriate activities that can accommodate the range of abilities and learning styles found in classrooms? (reading level, fine and gross motor skills)					
Cite evidence from the materials to support your rating.					
9. utilize a variety of instructional resources? (e.g., recommended list of trade books, measuring tools, information technology, manipulatives, primary sources, and electronic networks)					
Cite evidence from the materials to support your rating.					

(Continued)

(Continued)

To what extent do students' experiences …	Not at all	Inadequately	Adequately	Strongly	Exceptionally
10. focus on current scientific/mathematical knowledge that is accurately represented?					
Cite evidence from the materials to support your rating.					
11. provide opportunities for them to ask their own questions and conduct their own investigations?					
Cite evidence from the materials to support your rating.					
12. include assessment of their prior knowledge, embedded assessments, and performance measures?					
Cite evidence from the materials to support your rating.					
13. use real-world ideas, topics, and contexts that are appropriate and engaging for students?					
Cite evidence from the materials to support your rating.					

Source: © CESAME, Northeastern University, 1999

IMPACT Curriculum Review Panel
MST Instructional Materials Evaluation Tool

2. MATHEMATICS, SCIENCE, AND TECHNOLOGY CONTENT

To what extent do the instructional materials . . .	*Not at all*	*Inadequately*	*Adequately*	*Strongly*	*Exceptionally*
1. reflect the content standards of state frameworks or national standards? (Which document was used?)					
Cite evidence from the materials to support your rating.					
2. have mathematically and scientifically accurate and current content?					
Cite evidence from the materials to support your rating.					
3. use real-world contexts to develop science, technology, and/or mathematics ideas and topics that are appropriate and engaging for students?					
Cite evidence from the materials to support your rating.					
4. provide opportunities for students to work as a scientist, mathematician, or engineer?					
Cite evidence from the materials to support your rating.					
5. use language and illustrations that are free of bias and reflect the diversity of our society?					
Cite evidence from the materials to support your rating.					
6. emphasize depth rather than breadth in presentation of the content?					
Cite evidence from the materials to support your rating.					

Source: © CESAME, Northeastern University, 1999

IMPACT Curriculum Review Panel
MST Instructional Materials Evaluation Tool

3. ORGANIZATION AND STRUCTURE

To what extent do the instructional materials . . .	*Not at all*	*Inadequately*	*Adequately*	*Strongly*	*Exceptionally*
1. provide for in-depth, inquiry-based investigations of major scientific and mathematical concepts?					
Cite evidence from the materials to support your rating.					
2. provide cohesive units that build conceptual understanding?					
Cite evidence from the materials to support your rating.					
3. emphasize connections within and across disciplines?					
Cite evidence from the materials to support your rating.					
4. incorporate appropriate use of instructional technology? (e.g., computers, calculators, probeware)					
Cite evidence from the materials to support your rating.					
5. include activities that are safe with clear instructions on the use of tools, equipment, and materials?					
Cite evidence from the materials to support your rating.					

Source: © CESAME, Northeastern University, 1999

IMPACT Curriculum Review Panel
MST Instructional Materials Evaluation Tool

4. TEACHER SUPPORT MATERIALS

To what extent do the teacher support materials . . .	Not at all	Inadequately	Adequately	Strongly	Exceptionally
1. provide an overview of the content?					
Cite evidence from the materials to support your rating.					
2. provide suggestions to inform and engage parents and other community members?					
Cite evidence from the materials to support your rating.					
3. incorporate a variety of strategies to engage and stimulate all students? (e.g., open-ended questions, journals, manipulatives, visual, auditory and kinesthetic activities)					
Cite evidence from the materials to support your rating.					
4. provide a list of required instructional materials and reference useful supporting materials as appropriate? (e.g., videos, trade books, software, Web sites, electronic networks)					
Cite evidence from the materials to support your rating.					

(Continued)

(Continued)

To what extent do the teacher support materials . . .	Not at all	Inadequately	Adequately	Strongly	Exceptionally
5. suggest ways for teachers to adapt the materials to meet the needs of all students?					
Cite evidence from the materials to support your rating.					
6. give background information to support various learning approaches? (e.g., cooperative groups, student as teacher, independent research, learning centers, field trips)					
Cite evidence from the materials to support your rating.					
7. involve use of instructional technology to visualize complex concepts, acquire and analyze information, and communicate solutions?					
Cite evidence from the materials to support your rating.					
8. provide examples of student responses with rubrics to evaluate the assessments?					
Cite evidence from the materials to support your rating.					

Source: © CESAME, Northeastern University, 1999

IMPACT Curriculum Review Panel
MST Instructional Materials Evaluation Tool

5. STUDENT ASSESSMENT MATERIALS

To what extent are student assessment materials . . .	*Not at all*	*Inadequately*	*Adequately*	*Strongly*	*Exceptionally*
1. free of racial, cultural, ethnic, linguistic, gender, and physical bias?					
Cite evidence from the materials to support your rating.					
2. aligned with the student experiences?					
Cite evidence from the materials to support your rating.					
3. embedded in the instructional program? (found throughout the unit, not just at the end)					
Cite evidence from the materials to support your rating.					
4. varied; incorporating multiple forms of assessment? (e.g., oral and written work, student demonstrations, student self-assessment, long-range projects, tests and quizzes, teacher observations, individual and group assessments, portfolios and journals)					
Cite evidence from the materials to support your rating.					
5. focused on both the process and content of learning such as: predicting, modeling, making inferences, and reasoning? (not just on the final product)					
Cite evidence from the materials to support your rating.					
6. useful to provide information about student learning to inform the teacher's instruction?					
Cite evidence from the materials to support your rating.					

Source: © CESAME, Northeastern University, 1999

IMPACT Curriculum Review Panel
MST Instructional Materials Evaluation Tool

6. PROGRAM DEVELOPMENT AND IMPLEMENTATION

To what extent do the instructional materials	*Not at all*	*Inadequately*	*Adequately*	*Strongly*	*Exceptionally*
1. reflect current research on teaching and learning?					
Cite evidence from the materials to support your rating.					
2. provide access to information regarding the evidence of effectiveness?					
Cite evidence from the materials to support your rating.					
3. provide published materials that include suggestions, strategies, and models for successful implementation at the classroom level?					
Cite evidence from the materials to support your rating.					
4. provide published materials that include suggestions, strategies, and models for successful implementation at the school or district level?					
Cite evidence from the materials to support your rating.					

Source: © CESAME, Northeastern University, 1999

IMPACT Curriculum Review Panel
MST Instructional Materials Evaluation Tool

SUMMARY RATINGS

Curriculum materials_____ Date_____

Units/modules reviewed_____ Grade level_____

Review team member(s)_____

How well do the indicators in the individual sheets support the criteria?

1. **STUDENT EXPERIENCES** criteria:
   (underline one)
   (1) Not at all (2) Inadequately (3) Adequately (4) Strongly (5) Exceptionally
   Justification of your summary rating:

2. **MATHEMATICS, SCIENCE, AND TECHNOLOGY CONTENT** criteria:
   (underline one)
   (1) Not at all (2) Inadequately (3) Adequately (4) Strongly (5) Exceptionally
   Justification of your summary rating:

3. **ORGANIZATION AND STRUCTURE** criteria:
   (underline one)
   (1) Not at all (2) Inadequately (3) Adequately (4) Strongly (5) Exceptionally
   Justification of your summary rating:

4. **TEACHER SUPPORT MATERIALS** criteria:
   (underline one)
   (1) Not at all (2) Inadequately (3) Adequately (4) Strongly (5) Exceptionally
   Justification of your summary rating:

5. **STUDENT ASSESSMENT MATERIALS** criteria:
   (underline one)
   (1) Not at all (2) Inadequately (3) Adequately (4) Strongly (5) Exceptionally
   Justification of your summary rating:

6. **PROGRAM DEVELOPMENT AND IMPLEMENTATION** criteria:
   (underline one)
   (1) Not at all (2) Inadequately (3) Adequately (4) Strongly (5) Exceptionally
   Justification of your summary rating:

Source: © CESAME, Northeastern University, 1999

References and Further Reading

Chapter 2. Putting Curriculum at the Center of Science Education Reform

American Association for the Advancement of Science. (1999, September 28). *Heavy books light on learning: Not one middle grades science text rated satisfactory by AAAS's Project 2061.* Retrieved September 19, 2007, from http://www.project2061.org/about/press/pr990928.htm.

Ball, D. L., & Cohen, D. K. (1996). Reform by the book: What is—or might be—the role of curriculum materials in teacher learning and instructional reform? *Educational Researcher, 25,* 6–14.

Cavanagh, S. (2004, December 14). U.S. gets better showing on latest international math and science exam. *Education Week.* Retrieved October 2, 2007, from www.edweek.org. (Registration required.)

Cavanagh, S. (2006, May 24). NAEP science scores essentially flat except at 4th grade level. *Education Week.* Retrieved October 2, 2007, from www.edweek.org. (Registration required.)

Cavanagh, S. (2006, June 7). NAEP scores show few budding scientists. *Education Week.* Retrieved October 2, 2007, from www.edweek.org. (Registration required.)

Education Development Center, Inc. (2000). *EDC K–12 Science Curriculum Dissemination Center: Curriculum Profiles.* Newton, MA: Author.

Education Development Center, Inc. (2001). *Frequently asked questions and answers on science curriculum selection and implementation.* Retrieved September 19, 2007, from http://cse.edc.org/products/pdfs/faqCurrSelection.pdf.

Laguarda, K. (2006). *Curriculum as the leading edge of reform: The building of capacity and leadership by the Science Curriculum Dissemination Centers: Conference proceedings.* Washington, DC: Policy Studies Associates, Inc.

Michigan State University. (1996). *TIMSS United States: Summary of findings*. Retrieved September 19, 2007, from http://ustimss.msu.edu/summary.htm.

National Research Council. (1996). *National Science Education Standards*. Washington, DC: National Academies Press.

National Science Foundation. (1997, January 10). *NSF 97–20: Elementary, secondary, and informal education: Program guideline*. Arlington, VA: Author. Retrieved September 20, 2007, from http://www.nsf.gov/pubs/stis1997/nsf9720/nsf9720.txt.

Schmidt, W. H. (2003). *NSF supported instructional materials: Something new and something old*. Paper prepared for the 2003 NSF IMD Mathematics and Science Curriculum Developers Conference.

St. John, M., Heenan, B., Houghton, N., & Tambe, P. (2001). *The NSF Implementation and Dissemination Centers: An analytic framework*. Inverness, CA: Inverness Research Associates.

Tushnet, N., Millsap, M. A., Abdullah-Welsh, N., Brigham, N., Cooley, E., Elliot, J., Johnston, K., Martinez, A., Nierenberg, M., & Rosenblum, S. (2000). *Final report on the evaluation of the National Science Foundation's Instructional Materials Development Program*. Arlington, VA: National Science Foundation.

Chapter 3. Selecting Curriculum Materials: A Critical Step in Science Program Design

Brearton, M. A., & Shuttleworth, S. (1999). Racing a comet. *Journal of Staff Development*, 20(1), 30–33.

Laguarda, K. (2006). *Curriculum as the leading edge of reform: The building of capacity and leadership by the Science Curriculum Dissemination Centers: Conference proceedings*. Washington, DC: Policy Studies Associates.

National Research Council. (1996). *National Science Education Standards*. Washington, DC: National Academies Press.

National Science Resources Center. (1998). *Evaluation criteria for middle school science curriculum materials*. Washington, DC: Author.

Chapter 4. Professional Development for Curriculum Awareness, Adoption, and Implementation

Ball, D., & Cohen, D. (1999). Developing practice, developing practitioners: Toward a practice-based theory of professional education. In L. Darling-Hammond & G. Sykes (Eds.), *Teaching as the learning profession: Handbook of policy and practice* (pp. 3–32). San Francisco: Jossey-Bass.

Beyer, C., Delgado, C., Davis, E. A., & Krajcik, J. S. (2006). *Executive summary based on the final report for investigating high school biology texts as educative curriculum materials: Curriculum review process*. Retrieved September 21, 2007, from http://www4.nau.edu/cstl/cstl/site/prof_dev/prime/ExecSumInvestHSBioTexts.pdf.

Borko, H. (2004). Professional development and teacher learning: Mapping the terrain. *Educational Researcher, 33*(8), 3–15.

Carroll, C., & Mumme, J. (2001). *Leadership for change: Supporting and developing teacher leaders in mathematics renaissance K–12.* Retrieved September 21, 2007, from http://www.te-mat.org/Essays/caroll.aspx.

Cohen, D., & Ball, D. (1999). Instruction, capacity, and improvement. *CPRE Research Report*, No. RR-043. Philadelphia: University of Pennsylvania.

Cohen, D., & Hill, H. (2002). *Learning policy: When state education reform works.* New Haven, CT: Yale University Press.

Hirsh, S. (2004, Winter). Putting comprehensive staff development on target. *Journal of Staff Development, 25*(1), 12–15.

Loucks-Horsley, S., Love, N., Stiles, K., Mundry, S., & Hewson, P. (2003). *Designing professional development for teachers of science and mathematics* (2nd ed.) Thousand Oaks, CA: Corwin Press.

Loucks-Horsley, S., & Matsumoto, C. (1999). Research on professional development for teachers of mathematics and science: The state of the scene. *School Science and Mathematics, 99*(5), 258–268.

Loucks-Horsley, S., Stiles, K., & Hewson, P. (1996). Principles of effective professional development for mathematics and science education: A synthesis of standards. *NISE Brief* (National Institute for Science Education), *1*(1).

Peters, T. (2006, December 21). Personal electronic mail communication.

Sparks, D. (2002). *Designing powerful professional development for teachers and principals.* Oxford, OH: National Staff Development Council.

Stiles, K., & Mundry, S. (2002). Professional development and how teachers learn: Developing expert science teachers. In R. Bybee (Ed.), *Learning science and the science of learning* (pp. 137–151). Arlington, VA: NSTA Press.

Taylor, J. A., Van Scotter, P., & Coulson, D. (2007). Bridging research on learning and student achievement: The role of instructional materials. *The Science Educator, 16*(2), 44–50.

Willis, S. (2002). Creating a knowledge base for teaching: A conversation with James Stigler. *Educational Leadership, 59*(6), 6–11.

Chapter 5. The Role of Assessments and Accountability

Davies, A. (2003). Learning through assessment: Assessment for learning in the science classroom. In J. M. Atkin & J. E. Coffey (Eds.), *Everyday assessment in the science classroom* (pp. 13–25). Arlington, VA: NSTA Press.

Davis, M., Davis, S., & Hiles, E. (2005). *Evidence of understanding: An introduction to assessments in K–12 science curricula.* Retrieved September 25, 2007, from http://cse.edc.org/products/assessment.

Education Development Center, Inc. (2000). *EDC K–12 Science Curriculum Dissemination Center: Curriculum profiles.* Newton, MA: Author.

Hein, G. E., & Price, S. (1994). *Active assessment for active science: A guide for elementary school teachers.* Portsmouth, NH: Heinemann.

Love, N. (2004). Taking data to new depths: There's a ton of data being collected: The trick is to know how to use it effectively. *Journal of Staff Development, 25*(4), 22–26.

National Research Council. (1996). *National Science Education Standards.* Washington, DC: National Academies Press.

National Research Council. (2001). *Classroom assessment and the National Science Education Standards.* Washington, DC: National Academies Press.

National Research Council. (2003). *Assessment in support of instruction and learning: Bridging the gap between large-scale and classroom assessment: Workshop report.* Washington, DC: National Academies Press.

National Research Council. (2005). *Systems for state science assessment.* Washington, DC: National Academies Press.

St. John, M., Heenan, B., Houghton, N., & Tambe, P. (2001). *The NSF implementation and dissemination centers: An analytic framework.* Inverness, CA: Inverness Research Associates.

Chapter 6. Lessons Learned From Evaluation

Baldassari, C., & Lee, S. (2003). *NSRC LASER initiative: Final evaluation report.* Paper prepared by the Program Evaluation and Research Group at Lesley University Cambridge, MA.

Buonopane, D., Altobello, C., Atlas, T., & Storeygard, J. (2003). *Project IMPACT: Final summative evaluation report with in-depth studies of selected IMPACT Centers.* Paper prepared by the Program Evaluation and Research Group at Lesley University Cambridge, MA.

Laguarda, K., Funkhouser, J., Hildreth, J., & Kirkwood, K. (2003). *Supporting the adoption of exemplary science curriculum materials in underserved districts: Evaluation of the EDC K–12 science curriculum dissemination center.* Paper prepared by Policy Studies Associates, Inc.

St. John, M. (2002). *Investing in the development and dissemination of innovative curricula.* Presentation to the Gateways Conference, January 31, 2002. Retrieved September 25, 2007, from http://www.agiweb.org/education/nsf02/StJohnPowerpoint.pdf.

St. John, M., Heenan, B., Houghton, N., & Tambe, P. (2001). *The NSF implementation and dissemination centers: An analytic framework.* Inverness, CA: Inverness Research Associates.

St. John, M., Hirabyashi, J., Helms, J., & Tambe, P. (2005). *A summative report of contributions and impacts of the SCI Center.* Paper prepared by Inverness Research Associates.

Turnbull, B. J., & Laguarda, K. G. (2006). *The surprising challenges of knowledge use.* Retrieved September 25, 2007, from http://www.policystudies.com/studies/technical/Challenges%20of%20Knowledge%20Use.pdf.

Tushnet, N. C., Millsap, M. A., Stout, J. L., Johnston, K., Ormsby, C., & Martinez, A. (2002). *Instructional materials development dissemination and implementation: Site evaluation: Final report.* Paper prepared by WestEd and Abt Associates, Inc.

Chapter 7. Using the Centers' Work to Improve Science Education: Some Practical Advice

Laguarda, K. (2006). *Curriculum as the leading edge of reform: The building of capacity and leadership by the science curriculum dissemination centers: Conference proceedings.* Washington, DC: Policy Studies Associates, Inc.

Michigan State University. (1996). *TIMSS United States: Summary of findings.* Retrieved September 19, 2007, from http://ustimss.msu.edu/summary.htm.

Index

AAAS Project 2061, 16
Academic rigor of curriculum, 27
Accountability systems, 20, 85
Accountability testing, 55–58
Action steps, 78–83
Active learners, 13
Administrators
   assessments used by, 52
   description of, 39–40
   familiarity and comfort with
      instructional materials, 82
Analyzing Instructional Materials
   (AIM) process, 29–30
Assessments
   challenges associated with, 79
   EDC's K–12 Science Curriculum
      Dissemination Center, 52–55
   frontiers in, 51–55
   mandated, 85
   professional development
      effectiveness, 42
   resistance to, 55
   in science education programs, 13
   from standards-based curricula, 50
   state-based differences, 57
   summary of, 59
   teacher use of, 52, 59
   team acquaintance with, 52–53
   tools used to explain, 54–55

BSCS Biology, 15–16, 88
Buy-in, 32, 68

Classroom, 4
Curriculum
   change efforts, 65, 74
   "delivered," 9
   dissemination efforts, 8
   implementation of, 18
   inquiry-based, 55
   "intended," 9
   overhauling of, 10
   research-based, 55
   Schmidt's analysis of, 10
   school focus on, 17–21
   upgrading of, 76
Curriculum experts, 53
Curriculum leader, 31
Curriculum materials. *See also*
   Instructional materials
   adoption of, 65–70, 84
   district implementation of, 66
   education system, 80
   selection of. *See* Curriculum selection
   standards-based, 87–93
   state standards alignment with, 69
   teachers influenced by, 10, 47
   understanding of, 29
Curriculum selection
   academic rigor criteria, 27
   buy-in, 32, 68
   challenges associated with, 33
   coaching district teams through,
      25–26
   comprehensive approach to, 24
   developmental appropriateness
      criteria for, 27
   discussions before, 31
   district leadership support, 68
   EDC's K–12 Science Center process,
      27–28, 95–97
   equity criteria, 27
   evidence-based approach, 24
   foundation for, 30–33
   inquiry-based, 29–30, 78
   interventions to assist in, 33
   national science education standards
      as foundation for, 24

obstacles to, 33
pedagogical appropriateness, 28–29
professional development and, 35–36
professional learning experience, 32
summary of, 34
teams involved in, 25–26, 30–32
thought-based approach to, 25–30

"Delivered" curriculum, 9
Developmental appropriateness of
    curriculum, 27
Dissemination and implementation
    centers. *See also specific center*
  assessments, 56
  curriculum experts provided by, 53
  curriculum selection process
      emphasized by. *See* Curriculum
      selection
  demand developed by, 63–65
  description of, 17, 20–23
  district administrator participation
      in vision, 39–40
  evaluations by, 64–65
  local level involvement, 63
  professional development. *See*
      Professional development
  regional satellites, 62–63, 70–72
  strategies used by, 62–63
  support for, 77–78
  variations experienced by, 73
District administrators
  assessments used by, 52
  description of, 39–40
  familiarity and comfort with
      instructional materials, 82
District leadership, 68, 80
District teams
  curriculum selection by,
      25–26, 30–31
  evaluations about, 64
  as leaders, 31
  recruiting of, 63

EDC's K–12 Science Curriculum
    Dissemination Center
  assessment strategies, 52–55
  curriculum selection and evaluation
      process, 95–97
  description of, 17–18, 27
  evaluations by, 65
  regional capacity building
      efforts, 70–71
  training offered by, 58

Equity criteria for curriculum, 27
Evaluations
  EDC's K–12 Science Curriculum
      Dissemination Center, 65, 95–97
  regional satellites and, 62–63, 70–72
  Science Curriculum Implementation
      (SCI) Center, 67–68
  summary of, 72–73

Grade schools
  assessments in, 50
  instructional materials for, 14–15

High schools
  assessments in, 50
  instructional materials for, 15–16

IMPACT New England Center
  benefits of efforts by, 76
  Curriculum Review Panel MST
      instructional materials
      evaluation tool, 100–109
  description of, 19, 25–26, 38, 62–63
  regional capacity building efforts, 71
Innovation, 81
Inquiry, 13
Inquiry experiences, 39
In-service training, 36
*Insights: An Inquiry-Based Elementary
    School Science Curriculum*, 14–15
Insights in Biology, 67
Instructional materials. *See also*
    Curriculum materials
  adoption of, 65–70, 84
  Analyzing Instructional Materials
      (AIM) process, 29–30
  comfort with, 82
  demonstrations of implementation
      of, 53
  familiarity with, 82
  implementation of, 78–79
  *Insights: An Inquiry-Based Elementary
      School Science Curriculum*, 14–15
  learning based on, 9–10
  local use of, 57–58
  National Science Foundation,
      10–11, 13–14
  repeated exposures to, 79
  *Science and Technology Concepts for
      Middle Schools*, 15
  standards-based, 20–21, 43, 51,
      57–58, 87–93
  state standards and, 57–58

Instructional Materials Development
projects, 10–11, 13–14
"Intended" curriculum, 9
International tests, 7–8

"Job-embedded" training, 36

LASER Center
  description of, 28
  leadership institutes, 40
  learning communities built by, 40
  professional development efforts
    at, 45–46
  regional capacity building efforts,
    71–72
  regional partners, 66
Leadership, 41–42, 80–81
Leadership institutes, 40
Learning, 13
Learning communities, 40–41, 47
Licensure, 84–85

Middle schools
  assessments in, 50
  instructional materials for, 15

National Academy for Curriculum
  Leadership program, 19
National Academy of Science, 22
National Assessment of Educational
  Progress, 9
National Research Council, National
  Science Education Standards, 8, 11
National science education standards.
  See also Science education
  standards
  curriculum developed in accordance
    with, 24
  description of, 8, 23–24, 49
  goal of, 51
  instructional materials based on,
    20–21, 43, 51
National Science Foundation
  description of, 3
  dissemination and implementation
    centers. *See* Dissemination and
    implementation centers
  funding by, 21
  Instructional Materials Development
    projects, 10–11, 13–14
  progress by, 85
National Science Resources Center,
  3, 15, 19, 28

No Child Left Behind Act, 2, 8, 20,
  56, 82–83
Northern Indiana Science, Math, and
  Engineering Collaborative, 76

Pedagogical appropriateness, of
  curriculum, 28–29
Principals, 40
Priorities, 82
Professional development
  audiences for, 36, 43
  challenges associated with, 42–43
  curriculum selection and, 35–36
  definition of, 36, 79
  EDC K-12 Center, 39, 44
  effectiveness assessments, 42
  IMPACT Center approach, 38
  instructional materials as centerpiece
    for, 37–38
  LASER Center efforts at, 45–46
  leadership roles for teachers, 41–42
  local educators' involvement in, 43
  long-term strategies, 44
  needs of participants, 43
  resources to support, 69
  SCI Center approach, 38
  summary of, 46–47
  for teachers, 36–37, 39, 41
  training, 43–44
  variations in, 43, 79

Reforms
  initiation of, 3
  previous experience with, 69
  success in, 85–86
  time line of, 11–12
  types of, 2
Regional satellites, 62–63, 70–72
Research
  connecting with, 83–84
  curricula based on, 55
Resource groups, 82–83
Resources, 80
Rigor of curriculum, 27

Schmidt, William H., 10
*Science and Technology Concepts for
  Middle Schools*, 15
Science education
  conventional vs. innovative, 25
  decision making regarding, 4
  inadequacies in, 1
  present state of, 7

reforms in. *See* Reforms
status quo approach to, 1
Science education programs, 13
Science education standards. *See also*
   National science education
   standards
   curriculum materials based on, 87–93
   goal of, 51
   implementation of, 12
   instructional materials based on,
      20–21, 43, 51
   national, 23–24
   realization of, 12–14
   topics covered, 12
SCI (Science Curriculum
   Implementation) Center
   Analyzing Instructional Materials
      (AIM) process, 29
   assessment concepts and
      techniques, 52
   benefits of efforts by, 76
   description of, 19–20, 29, 38
   evaluations by, 67–68
   professional development reforms, 41
Standards. *See* National science
   education standards; Science
   education standards
State accountability systems, 20
State standards, 57
Statewide tests, 56
Substance, 77
Support, 77–78

Teachers
   assessments used by, 52, 59
   curriculum materials and,
      10, 39, 47, 79
   familiarity and comfort with
      instructional materials, 82
   inquiry experiences, 39
   in-service training for, 36
   leadership roles by, 41–42
   licensure of, 84–85
   preparation of, 17, 44
   pre-service preparation, 84–85
   professional development for,
      36–37, 39
Teams
   assessment concepts and
      techniques presented
      to, 52–53
   curriculum selection by,
      25–26, 30–32
Textbooks
   description of, 10, 85
   selection of, 17, 24
Third International Mathematics and
   Science Study report, 7–8
Training, professional development,
   43–44. *See also* Professional
   development

U.S. high school students, 7

Vision, 39–40, 47

The Corwin Press logo—a raven striding across an open book—represents the union of courage and learning. Corwin Press is committed to improving education for all learners by publishing books and other professional development resources for those serving the field of PreK–12 education. By providing practical, hands-on materials, Corwin Press continues to carry out the promise of its motto: **"Helping Educators Do Their Work Better."**

Education Development Center's mission is to enhance the quality and accessibility of education, health, and economic opportunity worldwide.

In compliance with GPSR, should you have any concerns about the safety of this product, please advise: International Associates Auditing & Certification Limited The Black Church, St Mary's Place, Dublin 7, D07 P4AX Ireland EUAR@ie.ia-net.com

www.ingramcontent.com/pod-product-compliance
Lightning Source LLC
Chambersburg PA
CBHW081359290426
44110CB00018B/2420